FAMOUS FURRY FICTIONAL FRIENDS

-The K-9 Edition-

By

Peter David Orr

BEACHFRONT PRESS

June 2023 Edition

Famous Furry Fictional Friends – The K-9 Edition/

Peter David Orr

ISBN 979-839765240-7

TABLE OF CONTENTS

Dug
Duke
Dynomutt, Dog Wonder
Eddie
Einstein ("Back to the Future")
Einstein ("Oliver & Company)
Fang (Harry Potter series)
Fang ("Get Smart")
Frank the Pug
Ghost
Goddard
Goofy
Gromit
Hachikō
Hercules (aka "The Beast")
Hong Kong Phooey
Hooch
Hot Dog
Huckleberry Hound
Jerry Lee
Jock
Krypto the Superdog
Lady
Ladybird
Lassie
Marmaduke
Max (Dr. Seuss character)
Max ("The Secret Life of Pets")
Moose
Mr. Peabody
Muttley
Nana
Odie
Old Yeller
Otis
Perdita
Pete the Pup (aka Petey)
Pongo
Poochie

Porkchop
Porthos
Precious Pup
Red Dog
Ren
Ribsy
Rin Tin Tin
Rowlf
Ruffles
Sam
Sam Sheepdog
Sandy
Santa's Little Helper (aka No. 8)
Scooby-Doo & Family
Scooter
Scud
Shadow
Slinky Dog
Snuffles (aka Snooper)
Spike & Tyke (Tom and Jerry)
Spike (Rugrats)
Snoopy
Snowball
Snowy
Spot
Sprocket
Stella
Strongheart
Tige
Toby
Toto
Tramp
Trusty
Underdog
Verdell
White Fang
Wishbone
Winn-Dixie
Zero

Introduction

Embark on a delightful journey through the lives and adventures of 90 famous furry fictional friends. From classic tales that have withstood the test of time to modern creations that have captured our contemporary hearts, this alphabetized compendium included a wide array of beloved characters from various mediums.

Whether they're found in books, comics, television shows, or movies, these fictional dogs occupy a special place in our hearts and imaginations. They are the heroes, companions, and loyal sidekicks who have left an indelible mark on our collective consciousness.

Each entry explores the unique traits, remarkable achievements, and origins of these iconic pups. You'll meet courageous canines who have saved the day, lovable companions who have brought joy and laughter, and faithful friends who have taught us the true meaning of loyalty. From the charmingly mischievous to the fiercely protective, these dogs reflect the vast range of personalities and qualities that have made them adored by generations.

Discover the heroic adventures of Ace the Bat-Hound as he fights alongside Gotham's Dark Knight or join the misadventures of Scooby-Doo and his mystery-solving gang as they unravel thrilling puzzles. Travel back in time to witness the heartwarming tale of Old Yeller or delve into the magical world of Harry Potter where the loyal Fang guards the halls of Hogwarts. These are just a few examples of the canine tales awaiting your exploration.

Whether you're a lifelong fan of these characters or an eager newcomer, this volume promises to be a captivating companion. It serves as a tribute to the enduring power of our canine friends' presence in our lives, reminding us of the unconditional love and companionship they offer.

So, find a cozy spot and allow yourself to be immersed in their adventures, moved by their loyalty, and inspired by their timeless tales. These legendary canines are waiting to capture your heart and leave an everlasting pawprint on your soul.

Ace the Bat-Hound

Ace the Bat-Hound is a beloved fictional character from the animated television series "Batman: The Animated Series." Ace, a loyal and courageous canine companion to Batman, is a German Shepherd who brings a unique blend of charm and tenacity to the show. Despite his non-human status, Ace is an essential part of Batman's crime-fighting team.

Ace possesses a striking appearance, with sleek black fur, piercing brown eyes, and a muscular build. His unwavering loyalty and unwavering dedication to Batman make him an invaluable ally in their relentless pursuit of justice. Ace's sharp senses and superior tracking skills aid the Caped Crusader in capturing criminals and foiling their nefarious plans. Beneath his tough exterior, Ace has a gentle and compassionate side, often providing comfort to Batman during challenging times. With his innate ability to understand Batman's unspoken commands, Ace is an indispensable and trusted partner in the fight against crime in Gotham City.

Apollo and Zeus

Apollo and Zeus are Doberman Pinschers who serve as loyal companions to Jonathan Higgins in the original Magnum, P.I. TV series. These magnificent dogs are known for their unwavering loyalty, intelligence, and exceptional training. Apollo, the elder of the two, has a sleek black coat and piercing, intelligent eyes. He possesses a calm and composed demeanor, always observing his surroundings with a vigilant yet gentle gaze. Zeus, has a bit more tan in his coat, and is the more vibrant and energetic of the two.

Jonathan Higgins, the owner and handler of "The Lads," as he fondly called them, regarded them as his trusted and valuable partners. He admires their unwavering loyalty and dependability, which have earned them a reputation as the best-trained dogs in the business. Apollo, with his wise and composed demeanor, is often the calm voice of reason, providing a sense of stability and wisdom to the group. Zeus, with his infectious enthusiasm and playful nature, adds a touch of excitement and joy to their adventures. Together, they form a harmonious trio, with Jonathan relying on their exceptional skills and fierce protectiveness to help protect the Robin's Nest, the luxurious Hawaiian estate which serves as the home base for the show.

The interactions between Magnum and Higgins's Dobermans involve a mix of tension, humor, and eventual teamwork, highlighting the unique dynamic between the characters and their shared devotion to protecting Robin's Nest.

One memorable interaction between Magnum, P.I. and Higgins's Dobermans on the TV show involves t Zeus in an episode titled "The Man from Marseilles." When Magnum finds himself taking care of Zeus after Higgins is unexpectedly called away. Initially, Magnum is somewhat apprehensive about being left alone with Zeus, and they have several comedic and tense encounters. For instance, Magnum attempts to go for a swim in the mansion's pool, only to find Zeus standing guard at the edge of the pool, growling at him, and refusing to let him enter. This playful standoff showcases Zeus's protective nature and his reluctance to let anyone trespass in Higgins's absence.

Astro

Astro is a beloved fictional character from the classic animated television series "The Jetsons." As a main character and a cherished member of the Jetson family, Astro captures the hearts of viewers with his endearing personality and unique abilities. Astro is a lovable and anthropomorphic dog, adding an element of charm and companionship to the futuristic world of the Jetsons.

Astro is a light grey Great Dane with a white lower face and expressive eyes. He often (but not always) stands on his hind legs, allowing him to interact with his human counterparts more easily. He possesses a wagging tail and floppy ears, which give him an adorable and approachable look.

Astro is incredibly loyal, always standing by the Jetson family's side, especially his primary owner, George Jetson. Astro's devotion is exemplified through his protective nature, as he goes to great lengths to ensure the safety of his family members. Whether it's alerting them of impending danger of being a steadfast companion during challenging times, Astro's loyalty is unwavering.

Astro's space-age collar allows him to communicate through a simplified form of human speech. Of course, the best-known phrase is "Ruh-Roh, Reorge!" Although Astro's words are often limited to expressing simple ideas and emotions, his ability to talk adds a delightful and entertaining aspect to his character. His voice is friendly and warm, embodying the persona of a loyal and dependable companion.

Astro's role in the Jetson family goes beyond mere companionship. He also takes on various household tasks, showcasing his versatility and helpfulness. Astro can be seen vacuuming the floors with a built-in cleaning attachment, fetching items, or even cooking basic meals for the family.

Astro has a playful and mischievous side, too, often engaging in humorous antics and adventures that provide comic relief in the show. His playful nature is particularly evident in his interactions with the youngest Jetson family member, Elroy, with whom he shares a special bond.

Astro embodies the idea that even in a futuristic world filled with technological advancements, the love and bond between humans and their pets remain timeless and cherished.

Augie Doggie and Doggie Daddy

Augie Doggie and Doggie Daddy are a lovable father-son duo from the classic Hanna-Barbera cartoon series. Augie, a young and energetic pup, is the son of Doggie Daddy, a wise and patient beagle. Together, they embark on humorous misadventures that revolve around the challenges and joys of their father-son relationship, capturing the hearts of viewers with their endearing dynamic.

Augie is a small, playful puppy with floppy ears and a boundless curiosity. He possesses a childlike innocence and a mischievous spirit that often lands him and his father in comical situations. Augie's zest for life and infectious enthusiasm brings a youthful energy to the show, while his unwavering love for his father serves as a heartwarming reminder of the strength of their bond.

Doggie Daddy, on the other hand, is a wise and patient father figure. With his distinguished voice and gentle demeanor, he guides Augie through life's lessons, imparting important life values. Doggie Daddy's calm and collected nature is a perfect complement to Augie's youthful exuberance, creating a harmonious balance between the two characters.

Balto

Balto is the courageous and compassionate protagonist of the animated film "Balto," a character that captivates audiences with his unwavering determination and heroic actions. Depicted as a half-wolf, half-dog hybrid, Balto possesses a striking appearance that reflects his unique heritage and sets him apart from the other sled dogs in the small town of Nome, Alaska. With his distinctive silver and gray fur, piercing blue eyes, and a powerful build, Balto's physical presence is as remarkable as his indomitable spirit.

The film, inspired by a true story, revolves around Balto's remarkable journey to deliver a much-needed antitoxin serum to Nome during the deadly diphtheria outbreak of 1925. Balto's wolf ancestry imbues him with exceptional strength, agility, and endurance, which proves to be invaluable throughout his challenging quest.

Balto's personality shines brightly as a blend of resilience, loyalty, and a gentle nature. Despite his outsider status and occasional ridicule from the other dogs due to his wolf heritage, Balto remains unyielding in his resolve to make a difference. He possesses a calm and introspective demeanor, observing the world around him with a deep understanding and empathy for others.

Balto's defining characteristic is his unyielding courage. When the sled dogs tasked with delivering the serum become stranded in a treacherous blizzard, Balto steps forward as their leader. Despite his self-doubt and uncertainty, Balto selflessly volunteers to embark on a perilous solo journey to retrieve the serum from a distant outpost. He exhibits remarkable bravery as he confronts various obstacles, including icy ravines, wild animals, and the relentless forces of nature.

Along his journey, Balto encounters a spirited and fiercely independent female husky named Jenna, who becomes his loyal companion and a source of encouragement. Their growing bond highlights Balto's capacity for deep connection and love, as he finds solace and strength in Jenna's unwavering belief in him.

Balto's journey is not only physical but also introspective, as he grapples with feelings of self-doubt and questions his place in the world. However, he discovers that it is his unique heritage and the strength within him that enable him to persevere and achieve extraordinary feats.

Balto's triumphant return to Nome, with the life-saving serum in tow, solidifies his place as a legendary hero in the eyes of the townspeople. The film beautifully portrays Balto's humility as he shies away from the spotlight, instead finding contentment in the knowledge that he has made a difference and saved countless lives.

Bandit

In the animated series "Jonny Quest," an adventurous young boy named Jonny embarks on daring missions with his father, Dr. Benton Quest, a renowned scientist. While Jonny, his father, and his friends face numerous perils and mysteries, they are accompanied by a loyal and courageous K-9 named Bandit. Bandit is a small, scrappy terrier, who is the faithful and trusted companion to the show's main character, Jonny.

Bandit's unwavering loyalty is evident from the very first moment he joins Jonny's family. He quickly establishes himself as Jonny's constant companion, offering unwavering support and a friendly presence. Bandit's loyalty transcends the ordinary bounds of a pet-owner relationship, as he becomes a confidant, protector, and friend to Jonny. Through thick and thin, Bandit remains by Jonny's side, lending a comforting presence and providing solace during times of danger or uncertainty.

Bandit's acute senses, perceptive nature, and ability to sniff out danger, uncover crucial clues, or detect hidden traps, make him an invaluable asset to the Quest team.

Bandit's bravery knows no bounds. Despite the perilous situations that frequently arise during their adventures, Bandit fearlessly charges into action, proving his mettle time and again. Whether facing dangerous wildlife, treacherous terrain, or sinister adversaries, Bandit remains resolute and unyielding. His unwavering courage inspires the team, reminding them to face adversity head-on with bravery and determination.

Barfy

Barfy is a fictional character from the post-apocalyptic novel and subsequent film adaptation titled "A Boy and His Dog." Set in a desolate and bleak future, Barfy is a loyal and resourceful canine companion to the story's protagonist, Vic.

Barfy is a medium-sized mutt with scruffy fur and a weathered appearance. He has a mix of brown and black patches covering his body, suggesting a combination of breeds. Despite his rugged exterior, Barfy possesses a bright pair of intelligent, amber-colored eyes that often reflect his alertness and understanding.

Barfy's personality embodies a unique blend of loyalty, cunning, and occasional mischievousness. He is incredibly protective of Vic, a young scavenger trying to survive in the harsh wasteland. The duo has developed a deep bond through their shared experiences and mutual reliance on each other.

One of Barfy's most notable traits is his exceptional intelligence. He demonstrates an uncanny ability to understand human language, interpreting Vic's commands and even responding with subtle gestures and sounds of his own. Barfy's communication skills go beyond mere comprehension; he can convey complex ideas and emotions through a combination of barks, whines, growls, and body language, making him a crucial companion and ally in Vic's dangerous world.

Barfy's keen senses and instincts play a vital role in their survival. He has an acute sense of smell, which helps him detect potential dangers, locate food, and uncover hidden resources. In addition, his sharp hearing enables him to detect subtle sounds, making him an excellent early warning system against threats. Barfy's agility and speed make him a formidable partner during confrontations, often assisting Vic in evading dangerous situations or ambushing unsuspecting adversaries.

Despite the harsh realities of their existence, Barfy manages to inject moments of lightness and levity into their adventures. His mischievous nature often leads to humorous situations, providing occasional respite from the bleakness of their surroundings. Barfy's antics create a sense of camaraderie between him and Vic, forging a bond that goes beyond mere survival.

Barfy's unconditional loyalty to Vic is unwavering, and he will risk his own safety to protect his human companion. Their relationship is characterized by trust, mutual dependence, and a deep emotional connection that transcends the post-apocalyptic world they inhabit.

Barkley

Barkley, the friendly and furry dog from the beloved children's television series "Sesame Street," is instantly recognizable and endearing. With his shaggy brown fur, speckled with patches of lighter and darker hues, Barkley is a charming mix of softness and playfulness. His large, expressive eyes shimmer with warmth and curiosity, drawing children and adults alike into his lovable world.

Standing tall and proud, this Muppet has a sturdy build, accentuated by a slightly stocky frame and a wagging tail that seems to have a mind of its own. His floppy ears, tipped with a lighter shade of brown, give him an air of approachability, while his mischievous grin showcases his friendly and playful nature. As Barkley bounds through the streets of "Sesame Street," his fur ruffles in the breeze, revealing its inviting texture, a testament to the countless hugs and snuggles he receives from his adoring friends.

Barkley's presence on "Sesame Street" brings an extra touch of warmth and familiarity to the diverse cast of Muppets and human characters. With each playful leap and wag of his tail, Barkley reminds viewers of the unbreakable bond that can be formed between humans and their furry companions. His appearance and demeanor make him a cherished and memorable character, leaving an indelible mark on the hearts of both young and old as a symbol of the joy and comfort that dogs bring into our lives.

Baxter

Baxter is a fictional character from the comedy film "Anchorman: The Legend of Ron Burgundy." The movie, set in the 1970s, follows the adventures of a group of eccentric news anchors in San Diego.

Baxter is a small and fluffy Border Terrier. He has a scruffy, wiry coat of fur that is predominantly tan in color. With his expressive brown eyes and endearing facial features, Baxter has an irresistible charm that adds to his appeal as a character.

Baxter's role in the film extends beyond that of a mere pet. He is portrayed as Ron Burgundy's trusted confidant and sidekick, always by his side both personally and professionally.

Baxter is known for his remarkable intelligence and ability to understand human speech. While he cannot speak, the film suggests that he has a deep understanding of human language, and that Ron Burgundy can understand every one of Baxter's barks, whines, growls, yelps, howls, whimpers, and grunts. Baxter often reacts to conversations with a range of adorable expressions and body language, as if he comprehends the discussions and participates in them on a non-verbal level.

There's a sequence is a sequence where Ron Burgundy is driving across a bridge with Baxter along for the ride, and Ron inadvertently causes a motorcyclist to crash by throwing a burrito out of the car window. The motorcyclist becomes angry and confronts Ron. As the situation escalates, the motorcyclist retaliates by punting Baxter off the bridge and into the water. This scene acts as the storyline's emotional nadir for Ron and as a catalyst for everything thereafter.

At the end of the film, it is revealed that Baxter did not die, and Ron and Baxter are reunited with awkward licks and kisses.

Beethoven

Beethoven is a beloved fictional K-9 character from the movie franchise of the same name. He is a lovable and mischievous St. Bernard with a heart as big as his droopy jowls. Beethoven first captured the hearts of audiences when the original film, "Beethoven" (1992). The character's popularity led to the creation of several sequels that further showcased his endearing personality and comedic adventures.

Beethoven is an imposing yet gentle dog. He possesses the classic traits of a St. Bernard, including a massive frame, a broad head, and expressive eyes that brim with warmth and playfulness. Beethoven's thick, long coat is typically a combination of white with patches of brown or tan, adding to his charming appearance.

What sets Beethoven apart is his delightful personality. He is incredibly friendly, and his affectionate nature endears him to everyone he encounters. Despite his large size, Beethoven is a gentle giant who is incredibly loyal and protective of his human family. He often acts as a guardian, keeping a watchful eye on the children and instinctively sensing when they are in danger or need his assistance.

Beethoven's mischievous side is also a prominent aspect of his character. He is known for his knack for getting into amusing predicaments that often result in chaos and laughter. From causing household mayhem to wreaking havoc during outings, Beethoven's antics never fail to bring smiles to the faces of both his on-screen family and audiences.

Bella

In W. Bruce Cameron's novel "A Dog's Way Home," the character Bella is not only a lovable and determined dog, but she also serves as a poignant example of the challenges faced by dogs, particularly those subjected to breed discrimination. Bella, a mixed breed dog with a gentle and intelligent demeanor, encounters the harsh reality of prejudice, particularly towards pitbulls, throughout her journey. The novel sheds light on the profound impact that breed discrimination has on the lives of both dogs and their owners, as Bella's story showcases the resilience and unwavering love that can transcend societal biases.

Throughout the novel and its film adaptation, Bella's experiences underscore the importance of challenging preconceived notions and stereotypes associated with certain dog breeds. Bella's own mixed heritage serves as a testament to the multifaceted nature of a dog's personality and the inherent unfairness of judging based on appearance alone. By depicting Bella's journey and the obstacles she faces due to breed discrimination, the story raises awareness about the impact of such biases on dogs' lives and the deep emotional toll it takes on their owners. Ultimately, Bella's tale serves as a reminder of the significance of acceptance, compassion, and understanding when it comes to embracing all dogs, regardless of their breed or appearance.

Benji

Benji is a lovable and intelligent canine protagonist who stars in the fictional K-9 movie franchise. This endearing character has captured the hearts of audiences worldwide with his charm, wit, and incredible abilities. With his trademark expressive eyes and playful demeanor, Benji has become an iconic figure in the realm of family-friendly films, leaving a lasting impression on viewers of all ages.

Benji is a small to medium-sized mixed-breed dog, characterized by his soft, fluffy fur, which varies in color from light golden brown to auburn. His expressive eyes are his most captivating feature. Benji possesses a lean and agile frame, allowing him to navigate through various environments effortlessly. His wagging tail and perky ears are always a testament to his cheerful and friendly disposition.

Benji is renowned for his unwavering loyalty, intelligence, and bravery. Despite his small stature, he possesses a huge heart and an unwavering determination to help those in need. Benji is compassionate, always going out of his way to offer comfort and support to those around him, both human and animal alike. He has an innate ability to understand and connect with people, often sensing their emotions and responding in a comforting manner.

Benji's exceptional intelligence and quick thinking make him a true asset in any situation. He has an uncanny knack for problem-solving and is known for his resourcefulness, often finding innovative ways to overcome obstacles. Benji's acute senses, particularly his keen sense of smell and hearing, allow him to navigate complex environments and detect danger or locate missing persons.

Despite his lack of formal training, Benji has acquired an impressive array of skills over the course of his movie adventures. He is an agile jumper, capable of leaping over fences and obstacles effortlessly. His stealth and ability to move silently make him a formidable ally, allowing him to outwit adversaries with ease. Benji is also an excellent communicator, conveying messages and warnings through a combination of barks, gestures, and expressions.

Benji's movies typically revolve around heartwarming stories that highlight the power of love, friendship, and perseverance. He often finds himself in challenging situations where he must use his intelligence and skills to protect and assist those in need. Whether it's rescuing lost children, helping elderly individuals regain their independence, or unraveling mysteries, Benji always rises to the occasion.

Blue

Blue is a beloved and iconic animated character from the children's television show "Blue's Clues." This adorable and inquisitive puppy captures the hearts of young viewers with her playful nature, problem-solving skills, and unwavering loyalty. As the main character and the show's canine protagonist, Blue engages children in interactive learning adventures, fostering their imagination and critical thinking.

Blue is a small, female, blue-colored puppy with big, expressive eyes and floppy ears. Her soft and fluffy fur is a vibrant shade of blue, which stands out against her white belly. Blue's animated features allow her to convey a wide range of emotions, from excitement and curiosity to joy and surprise. With her wagging tail and eager demeanor, Blue embodies the essence of a fun-loving and friendly companion.

Blue is known for her friendly and approachable nature, always eager to engage with her human friends and solve puzzles together. She is a patient and understanding character, offering support and encouragement as children explore the world alongside her. Blue is empathetic and perceptive, often using non-verbal cues to communicate her thoughts and feelings, making her relatable to young viewers.

While Blue is a puppy, she possesses remarkable problem-solving skills that help her tackle challenges and puzzles presented in each episode. Blue's keen observation skills and ability to think critically empower children to join her on interactive journeys, promoting cognitive development and logical thinking. She encourages children to make connections, identify patterns, and come up with creative solutions.

Blue's unique talent lies in her ability to leave behind "clues" throughout the show. These clues come in the form of paw prints, objects, or pictures, which she carefully places to guide children towards the answer to the episode's mystery. By engaging with Blue and following her clues, children learn valuable lessons about problem-solving, observation, and deductive reasoning.

"Blue's Clues" follows Blue and her human companion, Steve, who acts as the show's host, through various adventures and imaginative worlds. Each episode presents a specific problem or mystery that Blue and her friend must solve together. Blue's enthusiasm, coupled with her ability to leave clues, encourages children to actively participate in the narrative, fostering their cognitive and emotional development.

As Blue encounters different characters and environments, she teaches children about friendship, kindness, and empathy. Through her actions and interactions, Blue models positive behavior, such as sharing, taking turns, and expressing emotions in a healthy manner. The show's gentle pace, interactive elements, and repetitive structure create a safe and engaging space for children to learn and explore alongside their favorite blue puppy.

Bluey

Bluey is an anthropomorphic Blue Heeler puppy, known for her boundless energy, insatiable curiosity, and infectious zest for life. With her striking blue coat, speckled with patches of darker hues, Bluey stands out as a vibrant and playful presence. Her bright, sparkling eyes draw viewers into her imaginative adventures.

Bluey's compact and agile frame reflects her enthusiasm for exploration and play. Whether she's dashing across the backyard or engaging in imaginative games with her family, her animated movements showcase her joyful spirit. With each wag of her tail, Bluey exudes a sense of excitement and anticipation for the endless possibilities that the world holds.

Bluey's endearing qualities are not limited to her physical appearance. She embodies the values of family, growing up, and the rich Australian culture that the show celebrates. As she navigates various scenarios alongside her father Bandit, mother Chilli, and younger sister Bingo, Bluey's energy and imagination become catalysts for learning important life lessons and fostering strong family bonds.

Bolt

In the heartwarming 2008 computer-animated comedy-adventure film "Bolt," a fictional K-9 movie character takes center stage, capturing the imagination of audiences young and old. Bolt, a courageous and determined white German Shepherd, embarks on a thrilling and emotional journey that tests the boundaries of his reality and his unwavering loyalty to his human companion. This essay delves into the remarkable qualities, adventures, and growth of Bolt, establishing him as an unforgettable and iconic character in the realm of animated films.

Bolt's sleek and powerful body exudes an air of strength and agility. His crystal-clear blue eyes reflect both intelligence and unwavering determination. Bolt's appearance is enhanced by a bold, jet-black lightning bolt-shaped marking on his chest, symbolizing his extraordinary superhero persona. With each poised movement, his muscular form emanates grace and confidence, a testament to his exceptional physical capabilities.

Bolt's personality embodies a perfect amalgamation of unwavering loyalty, fierce determination, and a pure heart. His upbringing within the context of a fictional television show has shaped his outlook on the world, causing him to believe that he possesses superpowers. Despite this, Bolt's naivety is endearing, as he navigates reality with an unwavering belief in his abilities. He is fiercely protective of his human companion, Penny, displaying an unyielding dedication to her well-being and safety.

Bolt's heart is filled with an innocent curiosity and an unquenchable thirst for adventure. His experiences outside the confines of the television set challenge his perceptions and force him to confront the disparity between fantasy and reality. Through this journey, Bolt's character evolves, revealing a more profound understanding of himself and the world around him, while never losing the core of his unwavering loyalty and love for Penny.

Bolt's fictional portrayal as a superhero dog instills him with a remarkable array of abilities. His primary power is extraordinary speed, enabling him to dash and leap with unparalleled agility. Bolt's strength matches his speed, enabling him to overcome physical obstacles and opponents that stand in his way. He possesses acute senses, including heightened hearing and the ability to see in the dark, amplifying his awareness of his surroundings.

The most significant skill Bolt possesses, however, lies in his unwavering dedication to Penny. His immense love and loyalty towards his human companion enable him to perform extraordinary feats of bravery and protectiveness. Bolt's unwavering belief in his superpowers enhances his courage and determination, motivating him to confront any challenge that threatens Penny's safety.

Brian Griffin

Brian Griffin is a fictional character from the animated TV series "Family Guy." More than a "sidekick" on the show, he stands out as an intelligent, sophisticated, and often cynical member of the Griffin family. He possesses human-like qualities, including the ability to speak and engage in intellectual conversations. He is known for his love of literature, music, and a wide range of cultural pursuits. Brian often acts as the voice of reason within the dysfunctional Griffin household, offering witty observations and satirical commentary on the events happening around him.

Despite his intelligence, Brian sometimes finds himself caught up in his own flaws and vices. He has a weakness for alcohol and often struggles with his romantic relationships. Throughout the series, Brian goes through various career endeavors, including being a writer, a taxi driver, and even a politician, though his aspirations rarely go as planned.

Brian's relationship with the other members of the Griffin family, particularly his best friend Stewie, is a central aspect of his character. He and Stewie share a complex and unique bond, often embarking on adventures together and engaging in witty banter. Brian's friendship with Peter, the bumbling patriarch of the family, is a mix of camaraderie and exasperation.

Brian adds a level of sophistication and cultural references to the comedic world of "Family Guy." His human-like qualities and intellectual pursuits provide a contrast to the often crude and outrageous humor of the show. Brian Griffin is an integral part of the "Family Guy" ensemble, offering a mix of wit, charm, and occasional moral lessons.

Bruno

Bruno is a fictional character from the classic Disney animated film "Cinderella." He is a loyal and endearing bloodhound and serves as Cinderella's faithful companion and friend. Bruno is known for his gentle nature, protectiveness, and unwavering loyalty to Cinderella.

In the film, Bruno resides in Cinderella's home, a chateau, and is shown to have a close bond with her. Despite his size and appearance, Bruno is depicted as a friendly and good-natured dog, always ready to support and comfort Cinderella in her difficult circumstances.

Bruno plays a pivotal role in the story, particularly during Cinderella's transformation for the royal ball. When the wicked stepsisters tear Cinderella's dress apart, Bruno tries to defend her and, in the process, rips their garments as well. This small act of bravery showcases his loyalty and protective instincts towards Cinderella.

Aside from his protective nature, Bruno is also portrayed as being quite clumsy and somewhat comical. His larger-than-life personality adds moments of light-heartedness to the film, often providing a contrast to the more serious and dramatic elements.

Bruno's character represents the idea of unwavering loyalty and the bond between humans and animals. His presence in the story emphasizes the importance of companionship, friendship, and kindness, highlighting Cinderella's pure-hearted nature and her ability to befriend and connect with animals.

Buck

Buck, the brave and resilient sled dog from "Call of the Wild," is a character that captures the essence of strength and perseverance in the face of adversity. As the story unfolds, Buck undergoes a transformative journey that tests his limits and reveals his true character. With his striking appearance and powerful presence, Buck commands attention and embodies the spirit of the untamed wilderness.

Buck's physicality reflects his heritage as a St. Bernard and Scotch Collie mix. His thick, lustrous fur, a blend of deep brown and white, shields him from the harsh elements of the icy landscape. His keen, intelligent eyes, gleaming with determination and a touch of wildness, betray the resilience within him.

Through his trials and tribulations, Buck's transformation unfolds. He evolves from a pampered house pet to a rugged and independent survivor, adapting to the harsh realities of life in the unforgiving wilderness. Buck's strength and resilience are not only physical but also spiritual, as he learns to trust his instincts and reconnect with his primal nature.

Buck's character resonates with audiences as he navigates the challenges and adventures of his journey. His loyalty and unwavering spirit become a symbol of courage and determination, inspiring viewers to confront their own obstacles with resilience and fortitude. Buck's presence in "Call of the Wild" serves as a reminder of the indomitable spirit that lies within us all, waiting to be awakened in the face of adversity.

Buck Bundy

Buck, the lovable Briard from the sitcom "Married...with Children," adds a delightful touch of canine charm to the dysfunctional Bundy family. As a Briard, a French breed renowned for its large shepherd dogs, Buck boasts an imposing yet endearing presence. With his shaggy multi-brown colored, "lion cut" fur, and expressive eyes, he captures the hearts of viewers as a beloved family pet.

What sets Buck apart is his unique portrayal through voice-overs that reveal his inner thoughts. This clever narrative device allows audiences to experience the world from Buck's perspective, unveiling his humorous and often sardonic observations on the daily antics of the Bundy household. Through these insights, Buck becomes an integral part of the show's comedic fabric, offering witty commentary on the absurdities of family life through unconventional interactions with Al, Peggy, Kelly, and Bud.

Buddy

Buddy, the beloved character from the "Air Bud" film series, is a remarkable and heartwarming Golden Retriever who captures the hearts of audiences with his incredible athletic abilities and unwavering loyalty. He is an exceptional sports-playing dog and the central focus of the franchise.

Buddy's story begins when he is found by Josh Framm, a young boy struggling to adjust to a new town and school. From the start, Buddy and Josh develop an unbreakable bond, and it becomes evident that Buddy possesses a remarkable talent for playing various sports. He showcases his skills in basketball, football, soccer, baseball, and even volleyball, leaving audiences amazed and inspired.

Buddy's athletic prowess is extraordinary, and he becomes an integral part of the sports teams he joins. His ability to perform incredible feats on the field or court not only astounds the characters in the movies but also inspires them to push beyond their limits and believe in themselves.

However, Buddy's story is not solely focused on sports. The films explore themes of friendship, family, and overcoming adversity. Buddy's presence in the lives of the characters helps them overcome their personal challenges and teaches them important life lessons. His loyalty and companionship provide a source of comfort and support, particularly for Josh, who finds solace in their special bond.

Buddy's character represents the idea that with dedication, perseverance, and the support of loved ones, one can achieve remarkable things.

Bruiser

Bruiser, the adorable Chihuahua from the movie "Legally Blonde," is a beloved and memorable character known for his small size, big personality, and significant role in the story. Bruiser serves as the faithful companion to Elle Woods, the film's main character, and plays an important part in her journey of self-discovery and empowerment.

From the moment Bruiser is introduced, he and Elle share an unbreakable bond. As Elle faces challenges and stereotypes in her pursuit of attending Harvard Law School, Bruiser remains a constant source of comfort and support. He is always by Elle's side, providing unconditional love and companionship, even in the face of adversity.

Bruiser's presence in the film adds a touch of lightheartedness and humor. His small stature and charming personality create amusing moments, often serving as comic relief during the more serious or intense scenes. Bruiser's antics and occasional mischievous behavior bring joy to both the characters in the movie and the audience watching.

Beyond his entertainment value, Bruiser symbolizes loyalty and determination. His unwavering support for Elle underscores the importance of standing by those we care about, even when faced with obstacles or judgments from others. Bruiser's character also challenges stereotypes, showcasing that a small dog can have a big impact and contribute to the success of their human companions.

Throughout the film, Bruiser's relationship with Elle evolves, mirroring her growth and transformation. As Elle discovers her true potential and challenges societal expectations, Bruiser serves as a constant reminder of the importance of staying true to oneself and embracing individuality.

Bruiser from "Legally Blonde" has become an iconic character, loved by audiences for his charm, comedic moments, and heartwarming presence. His role in the story reinforces the values of loyalty, love, and the power of embracing one's unique qualities. Bruiser's character exemplifies the idea that true companionship knows no boundaries, whether human or canine, and that the support of a loyal friend can make all the difference in achieving personal and professional success.

Chance

Chance, the lovable and adventurous American Bulldog from the film "Homeward Bound: The Incredible Journey," is known for his spirited personality, boundless energy, and unwavering loyalty to his human family. He plays a pivotal role in the heartwarming story of friendship, resilience, and the unbreakable bond between pets and their owners.

Chance, along with his companions Shadow and Sassy, embarks on a treacherous journey to find their owners when they believe they have been abandoned. Throughout their incredible adventure, Chance's exuberance and playful nature provide moments of levity and humor.

Despite his initial impulsive nature, Chance's character develops and matures as the story unfolds. He learns valuable lessons about responsibility, bravery, and the importance of family. Chance's growth and transformation resonate with audiences, reminding them of the capacity for change and personal growth within each of us.

Chance's loyalty and devotion to his human family are unwavering, even in the face of danger and adversity. He exhibits a deep sense of protectiveness and determination, ensuring that his fellow animal companions and the people he cares about are safe and cared for.

As the film progresses, Chance's friendship with Shadow, the wise and older Golden Retriever, deepens, and they form a strong bond. The contrast between their personalities, with Chance's youthful enthusiasm and Shadow's calm wisdom, highlights the importance of teamwork and accepting each other's differences.

Charlie B. Barkin

Charlie B. Barkin, the street-smart and charismatic dog from the animated film "All Dogs Go to Heaven," captures the hearts of audiences with his rough-edged charm and spirited personality. Charlie's journey begins after his untimely demise, when he finds himself embarking on thrilling adventures in the afterlife.

Charlie's physicality reflects his street-smart persona. With a scruffy coat of fur, a mix of brown and tan hues, and a mischievous glint in his eyes, Charlie exudes a sense of cunning and adventure. His quick-wittedness and slick mannerisms make him a magnetic character, drawing others into his schemes and escapades.

While Charlie's exterior may suggest a rough exterior, underneath beats a compassionate heart. As he navigates the afterlife, he develops a sense of redemption and learns the value of friendship and sacrifice. Charlie's transformation from a self-serving opportunist to a loyal and caring companion adds depth to his character, resonating with viewers on an emotional level.

With his quick thinking and street-smarts, Charlie becomes a beacon of hope and inspiration for his fellow canine friends, showcasing the power of resilience and the capacity for personal growth. His adventures in the afterlife serve as a reminder that even in the face of adversity, second chances and redemption are possible, and true friendship can transcend time and space.

Chief

Chief, the older and wise Bloodhound from Disney's "The Fox and the Hound," is a character that exudes both strength and gentleness. As an experienced and seasoned hunting dog, Chief initially harbors skepticism towards the young fox, Tod, due to their contrasting backgrounds. However, over time, Chief's stoic demeanor gradually softens as he forms an unlikely friendship with Tod, showcasing the power of companionship and the capacity for change.

Chief's appearance reflects his noble lineage as a Bloodhound. With his large, droopy ears and a solemn expression in his wise eyes, Chief commands respect and radiates a sense of authority. His robust physique and distinct coloration, a combination of black and brown fur with hints of gray, highlight his maturity and wisdom. Chief's physical presence conveys a sense of reliability and stability, qualities that provide comfort to those around him.

Despite his gruff exterior, Chief reveals a tender heart beneath his tough demeanor. As he befriends Tod, Chief's protective instincts and paternal instincts emerge, leading him to become a guardian figure and a mentor to the young fox. Through their shared adventures and challenges, Chief's character evolves, and his loyalty and compassion shine through, breaking down barriers and demonstrating the transformative power of friendship.

Clifford

Clifford, from the beloved children's book series and animated television show "Clifford the Big Red Dog," is a fictional K-9 character who has captured the hearts of readers and viewers around the world. Clifford is not your average dog—his size sets him apart. He is an enormous, lovable, and friendly red Labrador Retriever who stands at an extraordinary height, towering over buildings and trees.

Originally a tiny puppy, Clifford grew exponentially due to a magical event. He was adopted by a kindhearted girl named Emily Elizabeth, who became his best friend and constant companion. Together, they embark on numerous adventures, spreading joy and teaching valuable life lessons along the way.

Clifford's immense size often leads to humorous and sometimes challenging situations. Despite his extraordinary proportions, Clifford possesses a gentle nature, always striving to be helpful, kind, and loyal. He demonstrates unwavering love and devotion to Emily Elizabeth and the people in their community, eagerly helping whenever they are in need.

Clifford's bright red fur is as vibrant as his personality, serving as a visual symbol of his uniqueness and boundless energy. His charming character and the heartwarming stories he stars in have made Clifford an enduring and iconic figure in children's literature and entertainment.

Through Clifford's adventures, children learn about friendship, acceptance, empathy, and the importance of embracing one's individuality. He embodies the idea that differences should be celebrated, and that with kindness and understanding, any challenge can be overcome.

Colonel

Colonel, the valiant K-9 character from Disney's "101 Dalmatians," is a true embodiment of loyalty and bravery. As a seasoned veteran and trusted ally, Colonel plays an integral role in the mission to rescue the kidnapped Dalmatian puppies from the clutches of the villainous Cruella de Vil. With his military background and unwavering dedication, Colonel commands respect and serves as a source of inspiration for the other canine characters.

Colonel's appearance captures the essence of a disciplined and courageous military dog. Standing tall and proud, his strong frame and muscular physique showcase his readiness for any challenge that comes his way. His sleek, black and white coat, meticulously groomed, adds a touch of elegance to his commanding presence. Colonel's piercing eyes, filled with determination and intelligence, reveal his unwavering commitment to protecting the innocent.

Beyond his physical attributes, Colonel's character shines through his unwavering loyalty and steadfast nature. His military training and experience instill a sense of discipline and order, making him a reliable and trusted leader among his fellow canine companions. Colonel's strategic thinking and quick decision-making skills become invaluable as he guides the rescue mission, ensuring the safety of the Dalmatian puppies and outsmarting the cunning plans of Cruella de Vil.

Comet

Comet, the lovable Golden Retriever, quickly became an iconic member of the Tanner family on the popular TV show "Full House." With his striking golden coat and a heart full of joy, Comet won the hearts of both the characters and the audience alike. Always ready for an adventure, he was the perfect companion for the Tanner kids, bringing an extra dose of love and laughter to their lives.

Comet's playful nature and boundless energy were truly infectious. He had a knack for brightening even the gloomiest of days with his wagging tail and contagious enthusiasm. Whether it was chasing a tennis ball, performing impressive tricks, or simply snuggling up with the family on the couch, Comet had an undeniable charm that could lift anyone's spirits. With his loyal and gentle nature, he quickly formed deep connections with each member of the Tanner family, becoming not just a pet but a cherished member of the household. Comet's presence in the show added an extra layer of warmth and happiness to the Tanner family dynamic, making him an unforgettable and beloved character in the hearts of fans around the world.

Copper

Copper, from the classic Disney film "The Fox and the Hound," is a fictional K-9 character that has touched the hearts of audiences since the movie's release in 1981. Copper is a loyal and courageous hound dog, known for his unwavering friendship and remarkable hunting skills.

The story revolves around Copper's unlikely friendship with Tod, a mischievous and adventurous fox. Despite their inherent differences and the societal expectations that dictate they should be enemies, Copper and Tod form a deep bond as young animals. They spend their days playing, exploring, and enjoying each other's company.

As Copper grows older, he becomes aware of his instincts as a hunting dog and the traditional role he must fulfill. This realization strains his friendship with Tod, as their contrasting natures and societal pressures threaten to drive them apart. Copper is torn between his loyalty to his best friend and his duty as a hunting dog, leading to a bittersweet and emotionally charged narrative.

Throughout the film, Copper's character exhibits loyalty, bravery, and a strong sense of duty. He is determined to protect those he cares about and demonstrates remarkable perseverance in challenging situations. Copper's relationship with his owner, Amos Slade, is also explored, highlighting the bond between a hunter and his faithful hunting dog.

Copper's appearance in "The Fox and the Hound" showcases the complex emotions that can arise from conflicting responsibilities and societal expectations. The character teaches audiences about the complexities of friendship, the importance of empathy and understanding, and the challenges of navigating one's place in the world.

"The Fox and the Hound" serves as a timeless reminder that friendship knows no bounds, even in the face of adversity and societal constraints. Copper's journey and his unwavering loyalty to Tod leave a lasting impression, illustrating the power of friendship and the capacity for change and growth.

Courage

Courage, the titular character from the animated series "Courage the Cowardly Dog," is a fictional K-9 character who has captivated audiences with his endearing personality and extraordinary courage. Despite his name, Courage is a small, pink, timid dog who finds himself in a constant state of fear due to the bizarre and often terrifying events that occur in his everyday life.

Living on a secluded farm in the middle of Nowhere with his elderly owners, Muriel and Eustace Bagge, Courage frequently encounters supernatural creatures, monsters, and otherworldly phenomena. Despite his natural inclination towards fear, Courage consistently rises to the occasion, displaying remarkable bravery and determination to protect his family from harm.

Throughout the series, Courage's unwavering love for Muriel and his deep sense of loyalty propel him into dangerous and frightening situations. He overcomes his own fears time and again, demonstrating immense strength of character and an unyielding desire to safeguard those he cares about. Courage's selflessness and willingness to confront his fears make him a true hero.

Courage's endearing traits extend beyond his bravery. He is known for his wide range of facial expressions, his distinctive voice, and his ability to communicate through exaggerated gestures. These qualities contribute to his charm and make him a relatable and lovable character for viewers of all ages.

The show's narrative often balances comedic moments with darker themes, emphasizing Courage's resilience and unwavering determination in the face of adversity. Despite the overwhelming odds stacked against him, Courage's bravery and resourcefulness often lead to unexpected triumphs, highlighting the importance of inner strength and resilience.

Courage's character embodies the notion that true bravery does not mean the absence of fear, but rather the ability to face fear head-on and push through it. His adventures in "Courage the Cowardly Dog" teach viewers valuable lessons about empathy, compassion, and the power of confronting and overcoming one's fears.

Cujo

Cujo is a massive Saint Bernard from the Stephen King novel and film by the same name, who is originally depicted as a friendly and lovable family pet. However, his life takes a tragic turn when he is bitten by a rabid bat, contracting the deadly disease. As the illness progresses, Cujo undergoes a drastic transformation, becoming a ferocious and relentless killing machine.

The film centers around a mother and her young son who become trapped inside their car, while Cujo, now driven by uncontrollable aggression, relentlessly stalks them. Cujo's physical strength, coupled with his menacing appearance, creates an atmosphere of terror and suspense throughout the movie.

Cujo's character serves as a symbol of the inherent dangers and unpredictability of nature, as well as the potential for darkness lurking beneath seemingly innocent creatures. His transformation into a terrifying force reflects the primal fears associated with the loss of control and the threat of violence.

While Cujo's portrayal is rooted in horror and the sinister side of the canine nature, his presence in the film highlights the potency of fear and the human instinct for survival. The character serves as a cautionary tale, reminding viewers of the horrors that can arise when ordinary circumstances take a tragic turn.

Despite his terrifying demeanor, Cujo's portrayal also evokes a sense of sympathy and tragedy. Once a beloved family pet, his descent into madness is a result of circumstances beyond his control.

Cujo stands as a chilling reminder that even the most loyal and familiar of creatures can become the embodiment of fear, terror, and the destructive potential within.

Daisy the Beagle

Daisy the Beagle is a significant and beloved dog character from the first John Wick movie. While Daisy's screen time is relatively brief, her impact on the story and the emotional connection she forms with the protagonist, John Wick, is profound.

Daisy is an adorable and affectionate Beagle with expressive brown eyes and a soft, tricolor coat. Her charming appearance perfectly complements her gentle and endearing personality.
Daisy's character is that of a loyal and beloved companion to John Wick. She is introduced as the cherished pet of John and his late wife, Helen. Daisy represents a symbol of love, warmth, and normalcy in John's life—a connection to the happiness he had before tragedy struck.

Daisy's presence brings moments of solace and tenderness to John Wick's world. They share quiet moments together, playing and cuddling, illustrating the bond of unconditional love between a human and their pet. Daisy's role serves as a reminder of the emotional support and comfort that dogs can provide during challenging times.

Tragically, Daisy's untimely demise becomes the catalyst for John Wick's relentless quest for revenge. Her death serves as a painful loss that sets off a chain of events, leading John Wick to re-enter the world of assassins. Daisy's significance in the narrative adds a layer of emotional depth and motivation to John's actions, showcasing the profound impact a beloved pet can have on our lives.
Daisy's character represents innocence, vulnerability, and the pure and unconditional love that dogs bring into our lives. Though her screen time is short, Daisy's presence leaves a lasting impression on both John Wick and the audience, highlighting the profound emotional bond between humans and their furry companions.

Daisy's portrayal in the first John Wick movie resonates with viewers, reminding us of the special connection we share with our beloved pets. She symbolizes the power of love and the lengths one will go to seek justice and find solace in the face of loss.

Deputy Dawg

Deputy Dawg, the charismatic anthropomorphic deputy sheriff dog, stole the hearts of audiences on the animated television series bearing his name. With his distinctive Southern drawl and a sheriff's hat perched on his head, Deputy Dawg brought a delightful mix of charm, humor, and law enforcement skills to the screen. Known for his quick wit and laid-back demeanor, he navigated the challenges of his job with a lighthearted approach that endeared him to viewers of all ages.

Deputy Dawg's calm and level-headed nature made him a reliable figure in his community. Despite the occasional mischief that came his way, he always maintained a strong sense of duty and responsibility. Whether he was solving crimes, mediating disputes, or facing off against his mischievous adversaries, such as Muskie Muskrat and Vincent van Gopher, Deputy Dawg approached every situation with a mix of cleverness and good heartedness. His interactions with other characters showcased his ability to find peaceful resolutions and diffuse tense situations, all while donning a charming grin and offering up witty one-liners.

While Deputy Dawg may not have been the most conventional law enforcement officer, his loyalty and dedication to upholding justice shone through in every episode. With his endearing personality and memorable catchphrases, Deputy Dawg left an indelible mark on viewers, reminding them of the power of kindness and a good sense of humor, even in the face of adversity.

Dodger

Dodger, from the animated film "Oliver & Company," is a fictional K-9 character known for his street-smart demeanor, charismatic personality, and loyalty to his pack. He is a charming and streetwise Jack Russell Terrier who serves as the leader of a gang of dogs living on the streets of New York City.

Dodger is introduced as a confident and street-savvy dog who takes the orphaned kitten Oliver under his wing. He becomes a mentor and friend to Oliver, showing him the ropes of survival in the bustling and often challenging urban environment. Dodger's protective nature and resourcefulness make him an integral part of their adventures.

Throughout the film, Dodger's character exudes a cool and carefree attitude. He is quick-witted, clever, and always ready with a snappy comeback. His charismatic charm and natural leadership skills inspire the other dogs in his pack, and they look up to him as their trusted leader.

Beneath Dodger's tough exterior, however, lies a compassionate and caring heart. He genuinely cares for his fellow pack members and is willing to go to great lengths to ensure their well-being. Dodger's loyalty to his friends and his willingness to stand up for what is right become key driving forces in the film's narrative.

Dodger's interactions with Oliver also highlight his capacity for empathy and his ability to form deep connections. He teaches Oliver the value of friendship, family, and belonging, while also imparting important life lessons about survival and self-confidence.

Dodger's character represents resilience and adaptability, showcasing the indomitable spirit that can arise from challenging circumstances. He embodies the notion that one's circumstances do not define their worth, and that friendship and loyalty can transcend social barriers.

With his catchy songs and memorable personality, Dodger has become a beloved character in the realm of animated canines. His presence in "Oliver & Company" contributes to the film's heartwarming themes of friendship, adventure, and finding a place to call home.

Dogbert

Dogbert, from the animated cartoon "Dilbert," is a fictional K-9 character known for his cynical wit, intelligence, and mischievous nature. He is a small, white dog with a sly grin, who happens to be the pet of the main character, Dilbert.

Dogbert is not your typical household dog. While he may appear innocent and harmless, he possesses a keen intellect and a razor-sharp sense of humor. He often serves as the voice of reason in the chaotic corporate world depicted in the cartoon, providing sarcastic commentary and clever insights into the absurdity of the workplace.

Despite his size, Dogbert exudes confidence and a self-assured demeanor. He is cunning and manipulative, using his intelligence to get what he wants or to expose the flaws and hypocrisies of the corporate environment. Dogbert's character is often portrayed as a charismatic schemer, offering unconventional solutions or sly advice to Dilbert and his colleagues.

Dogbert's dry humor and witty one-liners make him a fan favorite. He frequently delivers biting social commentary, satirizing the complexities and idiosyncrasies of office politics and bureaucracy. His character serves as a comedic relief, injecting levity into the often frustrating and absurd situations faced by Dilbert and his co-workers.

While Dogbert's personality may lean toward the conniving side, he occasionally displays moments of empathy and compassion, particularly when it comes to his owner, Dilbert. He has been known to offer guidance and support to Dilbert during his most challenging moments, showcasing a hidden depth to his character.

Dogbert's portrayal in "Dilbert" highlights the dichotomy between the mundanity of the corporate world and the cleverness of an animal who sees through its facades. He represents the inherent absurdities of corporate culture and serves as a reminder not to take everything too seriously.

Through his character, Dogbert offers a satirical commentary on the struggles and frustrations of the modern workplace, providing viewers with a humorous outlet to navigate the complexities of corporate life. His presence in the cartoon continues to resonate with audiences, striking a chord with those who can relate to the challenges of the nine-to-five grind.

Dogbert's combination of intelligence, sarcasm, and mischievous charm has made him an iconic character in the "Dilbert" universe. He represents the embodiment of a dog's unwavering loyalty to its owner, coupled with a sharp intellect that navigates the absurdities of the corporate world with biting humor.

Dino

Dino, from the classic animated TV show "The Flintstones," is a fictional character that has become an enduring symbol of the beloved Stone Age family's loyal and lovable pet to Fred and Wilma Flintstone.

Despite his prehistoric species, Dino exhibits many dog-like traits, including his unwavering loyalty, playful nature, and boundless energy. He is often seen enthusiastically greeting the Flintstone family with tail wags, slobbery kisses, and his signature "Snorkasaurus Snort."

Dino's character brings a delightful sense of joy and humor to the show. He is known for his exuberant antics, often getting into mischievous situations and causing chaos with his large size and clumsy demeanor. Yet, through it all, Dino remains an endearing and beloved member of the Flintstone household.

Dino's interactions with the other characters in the show, especially with his owner Fred, are filled with warmth and affection. He shares a special bond with Fred, always ready to provide companionship and lift his owner's spirits when needed. Dino's playful nature and ability to bring laughter to the Flintstone family and viewers alike make him an integral part of the show's charm.

While Dino doesn't speak human language, his expressive face, body language, and joyful noises effectively communicate his emotions. His character serves as a reminder of the unconditional love and companionship that pets bring to our lives, transcending the barriers of language and time.

Droopy

Droopy, the iconic cartoon character, made his first appearance in the animated series "Tom and Jerry." He is a fictional K-9 known for his calm and laid-back demeanor, slow drawl, and trademark droopy eyes. Droopy quickly became a fan favorite with his deadpan humor and unflappable nature.

Originally introduced in the "Tom and Jerry" shorts, Droopy eventually gained popularity and starred in his own spin-off series titled "Droopy." The show focused on the misadventures of Droopy, a lovable Basset Hound, as he navigated various challenges and encountered eccentric characters along the way.

Droopy's character is defined by his seemingly perpetual state of relaxation and tranquility. He rarely loses his composure, maintaining a calm and stoic presence even in the face of chaotic and unpredictable situations. His soft-spoken voice and slow movements add to his overall endearing charm.

Despite his unassuming appearance, Droopy possesses remarkable resilience and resourcefulness. He often finds himself in challenging circumstances, where he must outsmart his adversaries using his wit and intelligence. Through it all, Droopy maintains his cool and manages to outwit his opponents with clever strategies and unexpected bursts of energy.

Droopy's deadpan humor is one of his most memorable traits. His dry and understated delivery of punchlines and one-liners adds an extra layer of comedic effect to the cartoons. His ability to deliver hilarious lines with a straight face has endeared him to audiences over the years.

Droopy's portrayal often includes him as a hero, saving the day with his quick thinking and unexpected bursts of energy. Despite his initially unassuming appearance, he proves time and again that his unflappable nature and resourcefulness make him a formidable opponent or a reliable ally.

Droopy's character represents an archetype of calmness and wit in the face of adversity. His presence in the "Tom and Jerry" cartoons and his own spin-off series serves as a reminder that appearances can be deceiving, and that quiet determination can lead to surprising victories.

Dug

Dug, from the heartwarming animated film "Up," is a fictional K-9 that has captured the hearts of audiences with his lovable personality, unwavering loyalty, and endearing charm. He is a Golden Retriever with a special collar that grants him the ability to communicate through a device that translates his thoughts into speech.

Dug's character is marked by his infectious enthusiasm and eagerness to please. He is known for his bumbling and comedic antics, often getting easily distracted by squirrels and other objects of interest. Despite his scatterbrained nature, Dug's heart is always in the right place, and his loyalty shines through in every interaction.

One of Dug's most endearing qualities is his unwavering loyalty and desire for companionship. He attaches himself to the film's main characters, Carl and Russell, and becomes an integral part of their adventure. Dug's genuine eagerness to befriend and serve others showcases the pure and unconditional love that dogs are known for.

Dug's ability to communicate his thoughts and feelings through his collar adds an extra layer of humor and charm to his character. His simplistic and innocent outlook on life provides delightful comedic relief throughout the film. Dug's thoughts are often candid and lighthearted, offering hilarious insights into the situations and characters around him.

Beneath his comedic exterior, Dug's character also carries a poignant message about the importance of embracing others for who they are. Despite his occasional clumsiness and distractions, Dug's unwavering loyalty and unwavering commitment to his friends make him a cherished member of the film's cast.

Dug's portrayal in "Up" resonates with audiences of all ages. He represents the embodiment of a faithful and devoted companion, showcasing the unwavering love and loyalty that dogs offer their human counterparts. Dug's character has become an iconic symbol of the special bond between humans and their four-legged friends.

With his unforgettable catchphrase, "Squirrel!", Dug has become one of the most beloved and memorable animated K-9 characters of recent times. His infectious energy, pure heart, and comic timing continue to warm the hearts of viewers and remind us of the joys and love that our furry companions bring to our lives.

Duke

Duke, from the animated film "The Secret Life of Pets," is a K-9 known for his large size, playful nature, and journey of self-discovery. He is a lovable and boisterous Newfoundland dog who goes on an adventure alongside the film's main character, Max.

Duke's character is initially introduced as a new addition to Max's household, causing a bit of upheaval in their dynamic. He is portrayed as a big, slobbery, and sometimes unruly dog with a heart of gold. Duke's playful antics and his exuberant personality quickly make him a memorable and endearing presence in the film.

As the story unfolds, Duke's journey of self-discovery becomes a significant aspect of his character arc. Through his experiences with Max and their escapades in the city, Duke learns valuable lessons about trust, friendship, and finding one's place in the world. His character growth showcases the transformative power of unexpected friendships and the importance of embracing change.

Duke's portrayal emphasizes the joy and enthusiasm that dogs bring to our lives. He embodies the unwavering loyalty and unconditional love that dogs are known for, even in the face of challenging circumstances. Duke's relationship with Max evolves from initial rivalry to a deep bond built on mutual understanding and support.

Beyond his playful nature, Duke also demonstrates moments of vulnerability and tenderness. His backstory and insecurities add depth to his character, allowing audiences to empathize with his journey and cheer for his personal growth.

Duke's presence in "The Secret Life of Pets" contributes to the film's overall themes of friendship, acceptance, and the adventure that awaits beyond the comfort of our homes. He serves as a reminder that embracing new experiences and opening ourselves to others can lead to meaningful connections and personal growth.

Dynomutt, Dog Wonder

Dynomutt, Dog Wonder, is a K-9 character from the Hanna-Barbera animated series "Blue Falcon." He is a robotic superhero dog who aids the Blue Falcon, a costumed crime-fighter, in their mission to protect Big City from various villains.

Dynomutt's character is known for his energetic and enthusiastic nature. Equipped with an array of gadgets and gizmos, he possesses super strength, retractable limbs, and other special abilities that aid him in his crime-fighting endeavors. Dynomutt's loyalty and dedication to the Blue Falcon make him an integral part of their crime-fighting duo.

Despite his mechanical nature, Dynomutt exhibits many dog-like characteristics, including his playful and eager-to-please attitude. He often gets into comical situations, often resulting from his overzealousness or accidental activation of his gadgets. His endearing personality and humorous mishaps provide entertainment and comic relief throughout the show.

Dynomutt's interactions with the Blue Falcon highlight the strong bond and camaraderie between the two characters. He acts as the Blue Falcon's sidekick and trusted companion, always ready to assist and offer support in their crime-fighting endeavors. Dynomutt's unwavering loyalty and dedication make him a beloved character within the "Blue Falcon" series.

The show's lighthearted and adventurous tone, combined with Dynomutt's humorous and heroic escapades, made the character a memorable part of the Hanna-Barbera universe. Dynomutt's presence contributed to the show's overall appeal and popularity among viewers of all ages.

"Dynomutt, Dog Wonder" showcases the timeless appeal of the crime-fighting duo, where a canine companion and a heroic partner join forces to protect the city from evildoers. Dynomutt's character embodies the idea that heroes come in all shapes and sizes, and that even a robotic dog can make a significant impact with the right combination of heart, bravery, and technology.

Eddie

Eddie, the mischievous Jack Russell Terrier, became an instant fan favorite on the hit TV show "Frasier." Owned by Martin Crane, Eddie added a delightful dose of canine charm and unpredictable antics to the lives of the Crane family. With his scruffy fur and expressive eyes, Eddie quickly became an iconic and beloved character, earning his spot as one of the most memorable pets in television history.

Eddie's personality was as spirited as his appearance. Known for his independent nature and sly wit, he often found himself at the center of hilarious and unpredictable situations. Whether he was stealing the spotlight during a family conversation or engaging in playful banter with the show's titular character, Eddie never failed to bring laughter to both the characters and the audience. His ability to communicate nonverbally, with a simple tilt of his head or a knowing gaze, made him a scene-stealer, often stealing the thunder from the human cast members.

Einstein ("Back to the Future")

He's the loyal companion of the main character, Marty McFly, in the Steven Spielberg film "Back to the Future." He is a lovable and intelligent dog, named after the renowned physicist Albert Einstein.

Einstein is the first test subject for Doc Brown's time-traveling DeLorean car. As Marty McFly observes, Doc straps a device to Einstein's collar that will measure the precise moment when he reaches 88 miles per hour, the speed required for time travel.

Doc sends Einstein on a brief journey into the future. The suspense builds as the DeLorean races towards the designated time marker. Suddenly, the car disappears in a flash of light, leaving behind only fire trails in its wake. Moments later, the DeLorean reappears in the same spot, confirming that time travel is indeed possible.

Einstein emerges from the car, wagging his tail happily, seemingly unaware of the extraordinary feat he has just accomplished. The successful test not only showcases Doc's invention but also demonstrates Einstein's bravery and adaptability as the first living creature to travel through time.

Einstein ("Oliver & Company)

In the Disney animated film "Oliver & Company," Einstein is a lively and eccentric character, portrayed as a stray dog with a penchant for humor and a love for all things wild and wacky. He is part of a group of misfit dogs led by the street-smart Dodger.

Einstein is a Bullmastiff with a larger-than-life personality. He is physically imposing, with a stocky build and droopy jowls that add to his comical appearance. Despite his size, Einstein is portrayed as a lovable and friendly dog.

Einstein's defining characteristic is his boundless energy and enthusiasm. He is always ready for adventure and has an uncanny ability to find joy in the simplest things. Whether it's chasing his tail or playing with his fellow dog pals, Einstein is the epitome of exuberance.

While Einstein may not be the sharpest dog in the pack, he compensates for it with his kind-hearted nature. He is incredibly loyal and protective of his friends, always standing by them no matter the circumstances. Although he may not possess great intelligence, his playful and carefree spirit adds a touch of comic relief to the film.

Fang (Harry Potter series)

A memorable part of the magical world created by J.K. Rowling, Fang is a notable character in the Harry Potter series and belongs to Hagrid, the half-giant gamekeeper at Hogwarts School of Witchcraft and Wizardry. Despite his intimidating appearance, Fang is a loyal and kind-hearted creature.

Fang is a boarhound, a breed known for its large size and strong build. Towering over most humans, he possesses a shaggy coat that adds to his formidable presence. However, his size contrasts with his friendly nature, making him an endearing character throughout the series.

One of Fang's most defining traits is his unwavering loyalty to Hagrid. He is Hagrid's constant companion and is often seen by his side, faithfully following him wherever he goes. Fang's fierce devotion is evident in his protective nature, as he will do anything to ensure Hagrid's safety.

Despite his size, Fang is a gentle soul. He is known for his timidity and often gets scared easily, which adds to his charm. While some may mistake his fears for weakness, Fang's genuine heart and gentle disposition make him beloved by both characters and readers alike.

Fang's presence provides moments of comic relief throughout the series. His clumsiness and propensity to get into amusing predicaments inject lightheartedness into tense situations. Despite his occasional mishaps, his loyal and lovable nature endears him to the readers and the characters within the Harry Potter universe.

Fang ("Get Smart")

Fang, a recurring character in the classic TV series "Get Smart," is a faithful and courageous canine companion to Maxwell Smart, the bumbling secret agent known as Agent 86. Fang's role in the show is both comedic and supportive, adding an extra layer of humor and charm to the series.

Fang is a rough-haired sheepdog, known for his shaggy appearance and expressive eyes. Despite not having the typical traits of a spy, Fang proves to be an essential asset to Maxwell Smart and his crime-fighting missions.

Fang's loyalty to Agent 86 is unwavering. He is always by Smart's side, ready to assist or provide moral support in any way he can. Fang's steadfast presence highlights the bond between man and dog, and his devotion often adds an endearing touch to the comedic scenarios that unfold in the show.

In terms of his character traits, Fang is portrayed as intelligent and resourceful. While he may not possess the ability to speak or perform complex tasks, he often manages to save the day through his instincts and clever actions. Fang's contributions, though sometimes accidental, demonstrate his bravery and his willingness to protect his owner.

As a comedic device, Fang frequently finds himself in humorous situations that play off his dog-like behavior. Whether it's accidentally triggering gadgets or causing chaos during secret missions, his presence creates moments of lightheartedness and entertainment for the viewers.

One memorable and funny moment involving Fang in the TV series "Get Smart" occurred in an episode called "The Laser Blazer." In this episode, Agent 86 (Maxwell Smart) is on a mission to recover a stolen laser weapon.

During a crucial moment in the mission, Agent 86 finds himself trapped in a room with the laser device, which is set to activate and potentially cause significant harm. As Smart frantically tries to disable the device, Fang, who is with him, accidentally steps on a hidden pressure plate, triggering a series of booby traps.

In a comedic twist, the booby traps designed to hinder intruders end up targeting Fang instead. As the traps activate, Fang finds himself entangled in a net, triggering a cascade of pies to hit him in the face. The slapstick humor of the situation is heightened as Fang tries to free himself from the net, only to stumble and trip over his own paws, causing further chaos in the room.

Through the mishap, Fang unwittingly helps Agent 86 by inadvertently triggering the traps, distracting the guards and giving Smart an opportunity to disable the laser device. Despite the humorous circumstances, Fang's accidental involvement ultimately aids in the success of the mission.

Frank the Pug

Frank the Pug, the charismatic and talkative K-9 character from the film "Men in Black," left a lasting impression on audiences with his unique blend of wit, sass, and extraterrestrial expertise. With his compact frame, sleek black fur, and signature sunglasses, Frank quickly became an iconic figure in the world of science fiction. As the trusty informant and sidekick to the Men in Black agents, Frank brought both humor and crucial knowledge to their extraterrestrial investigations.

Frank's most striking feature was undoubtedly his ability to speak fluent English, adding an unexpected twist to the character. With his sharp tongue and witty one-liners, he often stole the spotlight in his scenes. Frank's sassy and confident demeanor, coupled with his vast knowledge of the alien world, made him an invaluable asset to the agents. He navigated the complex landscape of intergalactic affairs with ease, providing crucial information and a unique perspective on the extraterrestrial activities that the agents encountered.

Beyond his sharp wit and intelligence, Frank's loyalty to the Men in Black was unwavering. Despite his tendency to voice his own opinions and challenge authority, he ultimately remained a steadfast ally to the agents, offering his unique insights and unwavering support. Frank's presence in the film not only added comedic relief but also highlighted the importance of unconventional allies and the power of teamwork in the face of otherworldly challenges.

With his memorable appearance, quick wit, and undeniable charm, Frank the Pug left an indelible mark on both the "Men in Black" franchise and popular culture, proving that even a small, talking K-9 can play a big role in saving the world from extraterrestrial threats.

Ghost

Ghost, the loyal dire wolf, stands as a pitiable yet noble figure in the epic saga of "Game of Thrones." Born in the harsh lands beyond the Wall, Ghost's snowy white fur and piercing red eyes set him apart from his littermates, reflecting his uniqueness and his eventual journey as a misunderstood and often forgotten companion.

Despite his distinct appearance, Ghost often finds himself on the fringes of attention. While his siblings bask in admiration, commanding the respect of their human counterparts, Ghost is left behind, a mere shadow in the grand scheme of things. However, this doesn't dampen his loyalty or his unwavering commitment to his adoptive Stark family.

Ghost's most memorable moments stem from his steadfast devotion to Jon Snow, the illegitimate son of Eddard Stark. When Jon joined the Night's Watch, Ghost became his constant companion, a silent guardian whose presence spoke volumes. Ghost's piercing gaze and silent vigilance proved essential, especially during Jon's perilous encounters beyond the Wall.

One of Ghost's most iconic moments came during the Battle of Winterfell, where he fought valiantly against the wights, protecting Jon's flank as the Night King approached. Though wounded and outnumbered, Ghost fearlessly held his ground, embodying the spirit of House Stark and inspiring awe even in the face of certain doom.

Despite his valor, Ghost's plight continued. His loyalty was often overlooked, and he remained absent from critical events and gatherings, his presence felt only in brief, fleeting moments. While Jon faced battles and political turmoil, Ghost remained in the shadows, yearning for affection and acknowledgement.

It is in these moments of solitude that Ghost's true nature shines through. He embodies the essence of the dire wolves, ancient creatures bound by an unbreakable connection to the Stark family. Ghost's loneliness serves as a metaphor for the untold sacrifices made in the pursuit of duty and honor.

In the end, Ghost's character arc reflects the harsh realities of the "Game of Thrones" universe. Despite his unwavering loyalty and remarkable resilience, he remains a pitiable figure, often neglected and forgotten. However, Ghost's silent strength and the love he holds for his Stark family make him an enduring symbol of the indomitable spirit that persists, even in the face of adversity.

Goddard

Goddard is an iconic character in the animated TV show "Jimmy Neutron: Boy Genius." Designed and created by Jimmy Neutron himself, Goddard is a remarkable robotic dog with an array of advanced technological capabilities. With a sleek metallic exterior and glowing blue eyes, Goddard embodies the perfect blend of loyalty, intelligence, and playful curiosity. He is equipped with numerous gadgets and tools, making him an invaluable companion in Jimmy's adventures. Goddard's main purpose is to assist Jimmy in his scientific pursuits, providing him with support, protection, and even transportation. Whether it's flying, morphing into different forms, or simply providing comic relief with his endearing dog-like behaviors, Goddard is an integral part of Jimmy's team, showcasing the wonders of technology in the show.

As a character, Goddard is incredibly loyal and devoted to Jimmy Neutron. Despite being a robotic creation, he exhibits genuine emotions and a strong sense of companionship. Goddard is always by Jimmy's side, ready to assist and protect him whenever needed. His intelligence is evident through his ability to understand Jimmy's commands and respond accordingly. Despite being a technological marvel, Goddard often displays dog-like behavior, wagging his tail, panting, and even barking when excited or happy. This endearing blend of advanced technology and playful antics makes Goddard an incredibly lovable character. His presence adds a touch of whimsy and humor to the show, making him a fan-favorite among viewers of all ages.

Goofy

Goofy, the lovable and endearing klutz from the Disney universe, stands out as a figure of perpetual clumsiness and good-natured simplicity. With his trademark toothy grin, protruding ears, and infectious laughter, Goofy's charm lies in his innate ability to bring joy and laughter to those around him, despite his propensity for mishaps.

Goofy's memorable moments are often intertwined with his countless misadventures. Whether he's attempting to fix something around the house, embarking on a new hobby, or simply trying to navigate through everyday life, Goofy's clumsiness consistently leads to hilarious and unpredictable outcomes.

One of Goofy's iconic moments arises from his unwavering determination to master new skills, no matter how unlikely or impractical they may be. From surfing to skiing, fishing to golfing, Goofy dives headfirst into each endeavor with childlike enthusiasm, often resulting in comical disasters. Yet, his spirit remains unbroken, as he dusts himself off and cheerfully continues his pursuit of enjoyment, undeterred by his frequent failures.

Goofy's unyielding optimism and ability to find humor in even the most awkward situations endear him to both his friends and audiences alike. He embodies the idea that life's challenges should be met with a lighthearted spirit, encouraging us to embrace our imperfections and find joy in the journey, rather than solely focusing on the end result.

Despite his clumsiness, Goofy's heart of gold shines through in his unwavering loyalty and genuine kindness towards his friends, most notably his long-time pal, Mickey Mouse. Whether it's offering a helping hand or providing a shoulder to lean on, Goofy's caring nature transcends his humorous mishaps and solidifies him as a beloved and trusted friend.

In the end, Goofy's character arc celebrates the beauty of embracing our quirks and imperfections. His lovable nature reminds us that life's missteps and blunders can be transformed into moments of joy and laughter. Through Goofy, Disney invites us to find solace in our own humanity and discover the beauty in the clumsy, whimsical dance that is life.

Gromit

Gromit, the silent genius of the beloved "Wallace and Gromit" series, stands as a remarkable K-9 character, capturing the hearts of audiences with his intelligence, resourcefulness, and unwavering loyalty. Despite his lack of speech, Gromit's expressions and actions speak volumes, making him a memorable and endearing figure in the world of animation.

Gromit is a medium-sized, white-colored dog with a smooth, plasticine texture that adds to his unique visual style.

Gromit's face is perhaps his most expressive feature. He has large, round, and alert brown eyes that are filled with intelligence and curiosity. His eyes are framed by black eyebrows, giving him a perpetually thoughtful and observant expression. Despite his lack of a mouth or nose, Gromit's face manages to convey a wide range of emotions through his expressive eyes and subtle movements.

His ears, which stick out sideways, are long and floppy, giving him an endearing and somewhat comical appearance. They are often perked up, adding to Gromit's attentive and alert demeanor.

Gromit's body is sleek and well-proportioned, emphasizing his agility and grace. His limbs are slender and capable, allowing him to navigate through complex situations with ease. Although he doesn't possess traditional dog-like features such as a tail or a snout, his overall form retains a strong resemblance to a canine, albeit with a unique, anthropomorphic charm.

Gromit's most memorable moments stem from his exceptional problem-solving abilities. Whether it's saving Wallace from his own eccentric inventions or navigating through thrilling adventures, Gromit's keen intellect and resourcefulness often take center stage. His ability to analyze situations and find creative solutions showcases his brilliance, often outshining his human counterpart.

One of Gromit's iconic moments comes in the form of his unwavering loyalty to Wallace, his bumbling yet lovable owner. Gromit's silent dedication and unspoken devotion are evident in his constant vigilance and willingness to go to great lengths to protect Wallace from the consequences of his own well-meaning, but misguided, actions. Gromit's loyalty serves as a testament to the enduring bond between human and canine, transcending words and reinforcing the power of unspoken connection.

Throughout the series, Gromit's silent expressions convey a range of emotions, from exasperation to concern, humor to compassion. His expressive eyes and subtle movements give him a depth and complexity that captivates audiences, allowing us to understand his thoughts and intentions without a single word spoken. Gromit's ability to communicate without words emphasizes the strength of nonverbal communication and the profound impact it can have on relationships.

In addition to his intelligence and loyalty, Gromit's quiet demeanor and unwavering composure make him a steadfast figure amidst the chaos and whimsy that surround him. He is the calm in the storm, the anchor that keeps the adventures grounded. Gromit's quiet presence reminds us of the power of steadiness and the importance of maintaining a level head, even in the face of absurdity and unpredictable situations.

Hachikō

Hachikō, the beloved dog from "Hachi: A Dog's Tale," is a tale of unwavering loyalty and devotion. This remarkable Akita breed captured the hearts of many with his unwavering commitment to his owner and his remarkable ability to touch the lives of all those around him.

Hachikō's story takes place in the 1920s in Tokyo, Japan. He is adopted by Professor Parker Wilson, a kind-hearted and compassionate man. Hachikō's loyalty to his owner is unparalleled. Every day, he accompanies Professor Wilson to the train station and eagerly awaits his return in the evening.

Tragically, Professor Wilson passes away unexpectedly, leaving Hachikō heartbroken and confused. Despite the loss, Hachikō continues his routine, waiting faithfully for his owner's return at the station every day for nine long years. His unwavering commitment inspires and touches the lives of everyone who witnesses his dedication.

Hachikō's character is defined by his profound love and loyalty. He remains steadfast in his devotion to his owner, refusing to accept his absence. His gentle nature and unwavering determination demonstrate the depths of a dog's love and loyalty.

Hachikō's story is a testament to the incredible bond between humans and animals, showing the power of love, loyalty, and the enduring impact a single dog can have on an entire community.

Hercules (aka "The Beast")

Hercules, the legendary dog from the movie "The Sandlot," is a larger-than-life character with a heart of gold. He embodies strength, bravery, and an unexpected softness that endears him to both the characters in the film and the audience.

Hercules is introduced as "The Beast," an intimidating and fearsome English Mastiff who guards the neighboring yard, which contains a treacherous and legendary baseball eaten by the dog. The kids of the Sandlot view him with a mixture of awe and terror. However, as the story unfolds, Hercules's true nature is revealed.

Despite his fearsome reputation, Hercules is a gentle giant with a kind and protective spirit. He becomes a pivotal character in the film as he forms a unique bond with a group of young baseball players. Hercules shows unwavering loyalty to the kids, and they, in turn, grow to adore and respect him.

Hercules's character is marked by a juxtaposition of strength and vulnerability. His physical prowess is evident, but beneath his tough exterior lies a dog who craves companionship and affection. As the film progresses, Hercules's true nature shines through, showcasing his capacity for love and friendship.

Hercules's role in "The Sandlot" teaches the audience valuable lessons about prejudice and stereotypes. His initial portrayal as a terrifying beast serves as a reminder not to judge based on appearances alone. Through the friendship that blossoms between Hercules and the boys, the film highlights the transformative power of understanding and empathy.

Hercules's character is a beloved and unforgettable presence in "The Sandlot." He represents the bonds that can form between unlikely friends and the profound impact they can have on each other's lives.

Hong Kong Phooey

Hong Kong Phooey is the charismatic and crime-fighting protagonist of the animated TV series "Hong Kong Phooey." Despite his seemingly unassuming job as a janitor, Hong Kong Phooey is actually a highly skilled and resourceful canine hero. Clad in his signature red karate outfit and black mask, he brings a unique blend of humor, bravery, and martial arts prowess to the show. Hong Kong Phooey's secret identity is Penrod "Penry" Pooch, a humble janitor who works at the police station. While Penry may come across as clumsy and bumbling, his true potential is revealed when he transforms into Hong Kong Phooey to fight crime and protect the innocent.

As a character, Hong Kong Phooey is endearingly flawed, often stumbling into success through a combination of luck and his comical misunderstandings. He possesses a big heart and a never-ending desire to make the world a safer place, even if he occasionally messes up along the way. Hong Kong Phooey's martial arts skills are not perfect, as he frequently misinterprets the instructions from his faithful cat sidekick, Spot, leading to humorous situations. Despite these setbacks, Hong Kong Phooey's determination and optimism never waver, and he always manages to save the day in the end. His character embodies the classic archetype of an underdog hero, creating a delightful blend of action, comedy, and heartwarming moments in the series.

Hooch

Hooch, the lovable and slobbery dog from the film "Turner & Hooch," is a character bursting with energy, charm, and a heart full of love. With his distinctive appearance and unwavering loyalty, Hooch steals the show and captures the hearts of both the characters in the film and the audience.

Hooch is introduced as a French Mastiff, a large and drool-prone breed, and his physical presence alone is enough to command attention. Initially, he is seen as a bit of a troublemaker, wreaking havoc, and chaos wherever he goes. However, as the story progresses, Hooch's true nature is revealed.

Beneath his boisterous exterior, Hooch possesses a heart of gold. He forms an unlikely bond with Detective Scott Turner, the film's protagonist, after witnessing a crime scene. Despite their differences, Hooch becomes a faithful companion and a key ally in Turner's investigation. Hooch's unwavering loyalty and protective nature showcase the depth of his character.

Hooch's character is defined by his joyful exuberance and his ability to bring people together. He has a knack for melting hearts and breaking down barriers with his infectious enthusiasm. His antics and hilarious expressions often bring laughter and light to even the most challenging situations.

Through his relationship with Turner, Hooch teaches the value of companionship and unconditional love. Despite the challenges and messes he creates, Hooch's presence ultimately brings joy and purpose to Turner's life. Their bond serves as a reminder of the transformative power of love and friendship.

Hooch's character in "Turner & Hooch" leaves a lasting impression, thanks to his unique blend of charm, humor, and loyalty. He proves that appearances can be deceiving, and the true measure of a dog's character lies in their capacity for love and their ability to bring out the best in their human companions. Hooch's slobbery kisses and boundless spirit make him an unforgettable and endearing character in the film.

In the early part of the movie "Turner & Hooch," there is a hilarious and chaotic scene where Hooch, the mischievous dog, wreaks havoc in Turner's apartment. The sequence is filled with comedic moments and showcases Hooch's playful yet destructive nature.

The scene begins innocently enough, with Turner leaving Hooch alone in his apartment for a short period. However, as soon as the door closes, the mischief begins. Hooch immediately starts exploring his new surroundings with uncontainable excitement.

First, Hooch discovers Turner's neatly arranged bookshelf, which becomes an irresistible playground for him. With his wagging tail and clumsy paws, Hooch manages to knock down one book after another, creating a hilarious domino effect. Pages fly through the air as Hooch jumps and spins amidst the chaos.

As Hooch continues his rampage, he spots a plush toy, possibly one of Turner's prized possessions. Seeing it as the ultimate plaything, Hooch pounces on it, tearing it apart in a frenzy of fluff and fabric. The camera cuts to Turner's shocked face as he witnesses the destruction in disbelief.

Next, Hooch decides to explore the kitchen, where he discovers a bowl of freshly baked cookies on the counter. Unable to resist the temptation, he devours the entire batch, leaving behind crumbs and a guilty expression on his face. Turner's disappointment and disbelief add to the comedic effect of the situation.

Throughout the scene, Hooch's slobbery antics, his wagging tail knocking things over, and his obliviousness to the chaos he creates generate laughter. Turner's escalating reactions, from surprise to frustration, further contribute to the comedic atmosphere.

Hot Dog

Hot Dog is a beloved and mischievous character from the animated television series "Archie's Weird Mysteries." He is a loyal and adventurous anthropomorphic hot dog who is always by Archie Andrews' side, adding a dash of humor and charm to the show.

Hot Dog is a plump, smiling hot dog with a vibrant yellow bun and a rich brown sausage inside. He has big, googly eyes that express his wide range of emotions, and he walks on two legs, with his round feet wearing bright red shoes. Despite being a hot dog, Hot Dog is incredibly flexible and agile, often performing acrobatic stunts and daring moves that defy his sausage-like shape.

Personality-wise, Hot Dog is playful, mischievous, and full of energy. He is often the instigator of hilarious and chaotic situations, adding a comedic element to the series. Hot Dog is fiercely loyal to Archie, serving as his confidant and partner in solving mysteries. He has a keen sense of adventure and is always ready to embark on thrilling escapades alongside Archie and his friends.

Hot Dog possesses a clever and street-smart demeanor, which occasionally surprises those around him. Despite not being able to speak in human language, he communicates effectively through animated expressions, gestures, and occasional barks. Hot Dog's non-verbal communication skills make him a unique and endearing character, as he effortlessly conveys his emotions and intentions.

Hot Dog's presence is not limited to the sidelines, as he often finds himself in the thick of the action, displaying unexpected bravery and resourcefulness when confronted with danger. He has a natural talent for sniffing out clues and sensing impending danger, making him an invaluable asset to Archie's mystery-solving endeavors.

Huckleberry Hound

Huckleberry Hound is a beloved character from the classic animated television series "The Huckleberry Hound Show." He is an easygoing, friendly, and ever-smiling blue dog with a Southern drawl, capturing the hearts of audiences with his laid-back charm and gentle nature.

Physically, Huckleberry Hound has a distinctive appearance, with his light blue fur and a round, pudgy body. He stands on two legs, often wearing a dapper outfit, such as a bowtie or a hat, adding to his endearing personality. Huckleberry has a pair of kind, expressive eyes that convey his emotions and a perpetually cheerful smile that never seems to fade away.

Personality-wise, Huckleberry Hound is known for his calm and relaxed demeanor, often approaching life's challenges with a positive attitude. He exudes a friendly and warm presence, always ready to lend a helping hand or a listening ear to anyone in need. Huckleberry possesses a slow-paced, easygoing manner of speaking, reflecting his Southern roots and adding to his overall charm.

Huckleberry is a true gentleman with a heart of gold. He embodies kindness, honesty, and integrity, making him an admirable role model for viewers. Despite encountering various misadventures, Huckleberry maintains a cool and collected composure, finding joy in the simplest of things. He often uses his clever wit and resourcefulness to overcome obstacles, showcasing his intelligence and problem-solving skills.

Huckleberry Hound is well-loved for his musical talents as well. He is frequently seen playing a banjo and singing soulful tunes that further add to the show's nostalgic charm. His soothing voice and melodious songs create a soothing atmosphere, bringing a sense of relaxation and tranquility to both the characters in the show and the viewers at home.

Huckleberry's adventures often find him in different settings and occupations, from a sheriff in the Wild West to a detective or a sportsman. Despite the changing scenarios, Huckleberry remains the epitome of kindness and affability, always leaving a positive impact on those he encounters.

With his endearing personality and gentle nature, Huckleberry Hound has become an iconic character in the world of animation. He embodies the values of friendship, compassion, and resilience, captivating audiences of all ages. Huckleberry's Southern charm and unwavering optimism make him a timeless and lovable character, reminding viewers of the importance of kindness and spreading positivity.

Jerry Lee

Jerry Lee is a character from the movie "K-9," a 1989 action-comedy film. Jerry Lee is a highly skilled and energetic police dog who becomes the partner of the protagonist, Detective Michael Dooley, played by James Belushi.

Jerry Lee is a German Shepherd with a bold and fearless personality. He possesses exceptional intelligence and a keen sense of smell, making him an invaluable asset in sniffing out drugs and tracking down criminals. With his intense focus and unwavering determination, Jerry Lee is always ready to take on any challenge that comes his way.
Despite his serious and dedicated nature, Jerry Lee also displays a mischievous and playful side. He often uses his wit and cleverness to outsmart both humans and other animals, adding a touch of humor to the film. Jerry Lee's antics provide a delightful contrast to Detective Dooley's gruff demeanor, creating an entertaining dynamic between the two characters.

Jerry Lee's loyalty to his partner is unwavering, and he is willing to put himself in harm's way to protect Detective Dooley. Their bond deepens as they work together, eventually forming a strong and inseparable partnership. Jerry Lee's bravery, intelligence, and unwavering dedication make him an unforgettable character in the film "K-9," and a beloved companion to Detective Dooley.

Jock

Jock is an endearing Scottish Terrier and a beloved character in Disney's animated film "Lady and the Tramp." With his thick, wiry fur, bushy eyebrows, and a distinctive Scottish accent, Jock exudes charm and warmth. As a loyal and trustworthy friend to Lady and Tramp, Jock serves as a mentor figure, offering wisdom and guidance to the two adventurous canines. Despite his small stature, Jock possesses a brave and protective nature, always ready to defend his friends from any harm.

Jock's Scottish heritage is a prominent aspect of his character, adding a touch of humor and cultural richness to the story. He often regales Lady and Tramp with stories of his Scottish ancestry, proudly showcasing his tartan collar. Jock's wisdom is complemented by his warm heart, as he genuinely cares for the well-being of Lady and Tramp. He offers advice and shares his experiences, helping them navigate the challenges they face throughout the film. Jock's loyalty, kindness, and unwavering friendship make him an integral part of Lady and Tramp's journey, capturing the hearts of viewers with his endearing personality.

Krypto the Superdog

Krypto the Superdog is a character from DC Comics and various animated adaptations, including the animated television series "Krypto the Superdog" that aired from 2005 to 2006. Krypto is a superheroic dog who possesses incredible powers and is the faithful companion of Superman.

Krypto is a white-furred, anthropomorphic dog of the breed known as a Kryptonian dog, originating from the planet Krypton. Just like his owner, Superman, Krypto gains his extraordinary abilities from exposure to Earth's yellow sun. He possesses superhuman strength, invulnerability, flight, and heat vision, among other powers. Krypto's powers make him a formidable ally and an invaluable asset in the fight against evil.

Despite his impressive abilities, Krypto maintains a playful and lovable nature. He is depicted as being loyal, friendly, and highly protective of his human friends and family. Krypto's strong sense of justice and compassion drive him to defend the innocent and help those in need, even when faced with great challenges.

Krypto's character is often portrayed with a childlike innocence and enthusiasm, which adds a sense of charm to his superhero persona. He embraces his role as a superhero dog with great gusto, tackling each mission or adventure with boundless energy and an unwavering determination to do good.
Krypto's interactions with other animal characters, both heroic and villainous, bring an element of humor and light-heartedness to his stories. He forms bonds and friendships with various creatures, showcasing his gentle and caring nature, and often serving as a source of inspiration and hope to those around him.

Lady

Lady is a character from the classic Disney animated film "Lady and the Tramp," released in 1955. Lady is a charming and refined Cocker Spaniel who finds herself on a romantic adventure that changes her life.

Lady is depicted as a well-groomed and elegant dog with a silky, golden-brown coat and expressive eyes. She lives a comfortable and sheltered life with her loving owners, Jim Dear and Darling. Lady embodies grace and innocence, capturing the essence of a pampered pet.

Despite her privileged upbringing, Lady possesses a curious and adventurous spirit. She yearns to explore the world beyond the confines of her home, which eventually leads her to cross paths with Tramp, a street-smart and carefree mutt. Through her encounters with Tramp and other colorful characters, Lady experiences a transformative journey that challenges her beliefs and broadens her understanding of the world.

Lady is characterized by her kind-hearted nature and unwavering loyalty. She deeply cares for her human family, especially Jim Dear and Darling, and is always eager to protect them from harm. Lady's genuine love and devotion shine through her actions, whether it's defending her owners or befriending and helping fellow dogs.

Throughout the film, Lady learns important life lessons about trust, friendship, and acceptance. Her encounters with Tramp teach her to embrace the beauty of simplicity and to find happiness in unexpected places. Lady's growth is portrayed with a sense of grace and poise, as she transitions from a sheltered pet to a courageous and compassionate companion.

Lady's iconic scene sharing a plate of spaghetti with Tramp, while the romantic ballad "Bella Notte" plays in the background, has become one of the most memorable moments in Disney animation. It showcases Lady's ability to find joy and connection with others, regardless of their backgrounds or circumstances.

Lady represents loyalty, love, and the transformative power of friendship. Her endearing personality, combined with her elegance and inner strength, have made her a cherished and timeless character in the world of animated films, capturing the hearts of audiences for generations.

Ladybird

Ladybird is a beloved character from the animated television series "King of the Hill," which aired from 1997 to 2010. Ladybird is the loyal and beloved pet dog of the Hill family, adding a touch of warmth and charm to the show's ensemble.

Ladybird is a purebred Bloodhound with a distinctive appearance, characterized by her droopy face, wrinkled skin, and long, floppy ears. Despite her rather unassuming exterior, Ladybird possesses a gentle and endearing nature that makes her an integral part of the Hill family.

Ladybird's personality is portrayed as patient, loyal, and loving. She serves as a constant source of comfort and support to the Hill family, particularly to Hank Hill, the show's protagonist. Ladybird's deep bond with Hank is evident throughout the series, as she often seeks his companionship and provides him with unconditional love and unwavering loyalty.

Ladybird's character represents the stability and consistency of a loyal family pet. She is always there to provide solace and support during challenging times, serving as a source of emotional grounding for the Hill family. Ladybird's presence in the show underscores the importance of the human-animal bond and highlights the positive impact that pets can have on our lives.

While Ladybird doesn't have the ability to speak, her expressions and actions convey a range of emotions. Whether it's offering a sympathetic glance or wagging her tail in excitement, Ladybird's non-verbal communication adds depth to her character and enhances the emotional connection she shares with the other characters in the show.

Lassie

Lassie is a beloved character from the long-running television series "Lassie," which aired from 1954 to 1973. Lassie is a female Rough Collie who has become an iconic symbol of loyalty, intelligence, and heroism.

Lassie is depicted as a beautiful and regal dog, with a luxurious coat of fur and a distinctive white blaze on her chest. She possesses a keen intellect and remarkable intuition, which enables her to understand and communicate with humans in extraordinary ways.

Lassie's character embodies unwavering loyalty and devotion. She is deeply connected to her human family, often portrayed as the protector and savior of those in need. Lassie's heroic actions and bravery are showcased in numerous episodes, as she fearlessly faces dangerous situations to rescue and safeguard both humans and other animals.
Throughout the series, Lassie demonstrates remarkable intelligence and problem-solving skills. She is often shown using her intelligence to outwit villains or find solutions to complex problems, solidifying her status as a resourceful and capable companion.

Lassie's interactions with children are a significant aspect of her character. She forms deep bonds with the young members of her human family, becoming their constant companion and providing them with guidance and support. Lassie's presence is depicted as a source of comfort and security for children, embodying the idea of a loyal and protective friend.

Beyond her role as a hero, Lassie also represents the values of compassion, empathy, and love. She displays an unwavering sense of right and wrong and often acts as a moral compass in the show, teaching important life lessons to both children and adults.

Lassie's character has become an enduring symbol of bravery, loyalty, and the indomitable spirit of dogs. Her stories have captivated audiences for decades, inspiring generations with tales of courage and compassion. Lassie's impact extends far beyond the television screen, solidifying her place as one of the most iconic canine characters in popular culture.

The dog who portrayed Lassie in the television series and several Lassie movies was a Rough Collie named Pal. Pal, born in 1940, was the first dog to take on the role of Lassie and became synonymous with the beloved character.

Pal was discovered by animal trainer Rudd Weatherwax, who recognized his potential to embody the intelligence, beauty, and spirit of Lassie. Pal's natural grace, expressive eyes, and majestic appearance made him a perfect fit for the role.

Pal's training under Weatherwax's guidance helped shape him into a talented and highly skilled performer. He learned an impressive array of commands and behaviors, showcasing his intelligence and ability to communicate with humans. His remarkable performance on-screen captivated audiences, elevating the character of Lassie to new heights.

Pal's portrayal of Lassie earned him great acclaim and popularity, making him one of the most famous canine actors in Hollywood history. He starred in the original "Lassie" television series for its first seven seasons and continued to make appearances in subsequent Lassie films and specials.

Marmaduke

Marmaduke is a character from the cartoon strip "Marmaduke," created by Brad Anderson in 1954. Marmaduke is a large and lovable Great Dane who brings chaos and laughter to the Winslow family's lives in his own unique way.

Marmaduke's physical appearance is characterized by his massive size, droopy jowls, and expressive eyes. Despite his imposing stature, Marmaduke has a gentle and friendly nature, making him approachable and endearing to both his family and readers of the comic strip.

Marmaduke's personality can be described as mischievous, free-spirited, and full of zest for life. He possesses a playful and adventurous spirit, often getting into amusing predicaments that result in comic mayhem. Marmaduke's antics and exuberance bring joy and laughter to the strip, creating humorous situations and lighthearted moments.

Marmaduke's relationships with the human characters in the strip, particularly the Winslow family, are central to his character. He forms deep bonds with the family members, often seeking their attention and companionship. Marmaduke's loyalty and affection are unwavering, and he is always there to provide comfort and support, even if it means inadvertently causing chaos in the process.

One of Marmaduke's defining traits is his insatiable appetite. He is notorious for his love of food, often leading to comedic situations as he attempts to satisfy his enormous hunger. Marmaduke's insatiable appetite becomes a recurring theme in the strip, adding an element of humor and relatability to his character.

Marmaduke's adventures and misadventures serve as a source of entertainment and a reflection of the everyday joys and challenges of pet ownership.

Max (Dr. Seuss character)

Max is a character from the beloved Dr. Seuss book and subsequent adaptations, including the animated television special "How the Grinch Stole Christmas!" Max is the faithful and loyal dog companion of the Grinch, adding heart and charm to the story.

Max is depicted as a small, scruffy, and endearing dog with shaggy fur and expressive eyes. He is the Grinch's only companion on Mount Crumpit, sharing the solitude of the Grinch's cave and the mischievous adventures that unfold.

Max's character embodies unwavering loyalty and unconditional love. Despite the Grinch's grumpy and mean-spirited demeanor, Max remains by his side, faithfully supporting and following his every command. Max's unwavering devotion highlights the power of love and loyalty, even in the face of adversity.

Max's interactions with the Grinch bring both humor and heart to the story. He often finds himself entangled in the Grinch's schemes, whether it's pulling the Grinch's sleigh or donning reindeer antlers to help with the Grinch's plan to steal Christmas. Max's innocence and willingness to go along with the Grinch's antics add a touch of comedy and warmth to the narrative.

Max's character also serves as a contrast to the Grinch's cold-heartedness. He embodies the spirit of joy, compassion, and acceptance, demonstrating that kindness can flourish even in the most unlikely of places. Max's presence serves as a reminder that love and friendship can soften even the grumpiest of hearts.

Max's transformation from a simple companion to an instrument of redemption for the Grinch is a testament to his unwavering loyalty and the power of love. He plays a vital role in the Grinch's change of heart, highlighting the transformative power of compassion and the importance of genuine connections.

Max has become an endearing and memorable character in the world of Dr. Seuss. His depiction as a loyal and loving companion reinforces the values of friendship, kindness, and the capacity for change within us all. Max's presence adds depth, heart, and a touch of canine charm to the timeless tale of the Grinch.

Max ("The Secret Life of Pets")

Max is a character from the animated film "The Secret Life of Pets," released in 2016. Max is a lovable and energetic Jack Russell Terrier who takes audiences on a comedic and heartwarming adventure exploring the secret lives of pets.

Max is depicted as a small and spirited dog with a wiry coat, expressive eyes, and a distinctive personality. He lives a happy and content life with his owner, Katie, and enjoys a close bond with her. Max's vibrant and playful nature is infectious, capturing the essence of a typical household pet bursting with energy and enthusiasm.

Max's character embodies loyalty, love, and a deep sense of protectiveness towards his owner. He is shown as a devoted companion who would do anything to keep Katie safe and happy. Max's unwavering dedication to Katie forms the core of his character, driving him to embark on a daring adventure when he believes she is in danger.

Throughout the film, Max experiences a journey of self-discovery and learns valuable lessons about friendship and acceptance. His world is turned upside down when he encounters Duke, a large and boisterous dog who becomes his reluctant roommate. Through their initially tumultuous relationship, Max learns the importance of embracing differences and the transformative power of genuine friendship.

Max's character is known for his witty and often humorous commentary on the secret lives of pets. He provides a voice for the audience as they uncover the hidden adventures and quirks of household animals, injecting levity and entertainment into the story.

Max's animated expressions and physical comedy add to his charm and relatability, appealing to both children and adults. His mischievous nature and ability to find himself in amusing situations create laughs and moments of levity throughout the film.

Max's journey in "The Secret Life of Pets" highlights the emotional depth and love that animals bring into our lives. His character reminds audiences of the joy, loyalty, and companionship that pets offer, tapping into the universal affection for our furry friends.

Moose

Moose is a character from the film "My Dog Skip," released in 2000. Moose, a Jack Russell Terrier, brings heart, companionship, and a sense of adventure to the story set in the 1940s.

Moose's physical appearance is that of a small and energetic Jack Russell Terrier with a wiry coat, perky ears, and bright, intelligent eyes. His compact size and boundless energy make him an ideal companion for the young protagonist, Willie Morris.

Moose's character is portrayed as an intelligent, loyal, and playful dog. He becomes Willie's best friend and confidant, guiding him through the ups and downs of childhood. Moose's unwavering loyalty and unconditional love create a profound bond with Willie, giving him the courage to navigate the challenges of growing up.

Moose's adventures with Willie form the backbone of the story. Together, they embark on various escapades, from playing catch to exploring the neighborhood. Moose's enthusiastic and fearless nature inspires Willie to step out of his comfort zone, teaching him valuable life lessons about courage, friendship, and responsibility.

Moose's presence also symbolizes the innocence and purity of childhood. As Willie's constant companion, Moose represents the unwavering support and companionship that a beloved pet can provide during pivotal moments of a person's life. He becomes an embodiment of the joy, love, and adventure that comes with the bond between a young child and their dog.

Throughout the film, Moose's character serves as a source of comic relief, showcasing his mischievous and playful nature. His high energy and humorous antics create light-hearted moments that add levity to the narrative.

Mr. Peabody

Created by animator-producers, Jay Ward and Alex Anderson, Mr. Peabody is an anthropomorphic dog who lives in a New York City penthouse with his adopted human son, Sherman. He originated as a character in the classic animated television series "The Rocky and Bullwinkle Show" in the 1960s. The show featured a segment called "Peabody's Improbable History" in which Mr. Peabody and his boy companion, Sherman, would travel back in time using the WABAC machine.

In the original cartoons, Mr. Peabody was depicted as a highly intelligent, bespectacled dog with a refined demeanor. He would educate Sherman about historical events by taking him on adventurous journeys to meet famous figures from the past. These animated segments became iconic for their humor, clever writing, and educational value.

The film "Mr. Peabody & Sherman," released in 2014, paid homage to the classic cartoon while expanding on the characters and their adventures. The movie introduced a deeper exploration of Mr. Peabody's character, his relationship with Sherman, and their time-traveling escapades.

Mr. Peabody's physical appearance is that of a white, bespectacled, and anthropomorphic dog. He exudes an air of sophistication, always impeccably dressed and exuding an aura of intelligence and confidence.

Mr. Peabody's character is defined by his exceptional intellect, problem-solving skills, and love for knowledge. He is a polymath with expertise ranging from science and literature to history and music. His vast knowledge and ingenuity enable him to invent groundbreaking devices and solve complex puzzles.

Despite his brilliance, Mr. Peabody remains grounded and compassionate. He takes on the role of a mentor and father figure to Sherman, a young boy he has adopted. Mr. Peabody's guidance and nurturing nature highlight his commitment to Sherman's well-being and education.

Mr. Peabody's time-traveling adventures with Sherman form the core of the film's narrative.

Beneath Mr. Peabody's intellectual prowess lies a heartfelt longing for genuine connections and acceptance. As a dog living in a human world, he faces challenges and prejudices, but his compassionate nature and unwavering loyalty to Sherman serve as a reminder of the universal power of love and family.

Mr. Peabody's character is known for his dry wit, clever wordplay, and sharp sense of humor. His quick thinking and ability to deliver humorous one-liners add levity to the story, captivating audiences of all ages.

Through his character, Mr. Peabody represents the idea that intelligence, curiosity, and kindness can coexist. He showcases the power of knowledge and the importance of using it for the betterment of others. Mr. Peabody's character demonstrates that being smart doesn't mean being distant or aloof but rather embracing the world with open arms and an empathetic heart.

Muttley

Muttley is a character from the animated series "Wacky Races," which aired in the late 1960s. Muttley is a small and scruffy mixed-breed dog with a distinctive wheezy laugh that has become one of his most memorable traits.

Muttley's physical appearance is characterized by his shaggy fur, droopy ears, and perpetual mischievous grin. His expressive eyes often convey his sly and cunning nature. Muttley is known for his distinctive snickering laugh, which he lets out whenever he witnesses mishaps or when he comes up with his own devious plans.

Muttley's personality can be described as conniving, cunning, and somewhat lazy. He is often seen as the sidekick and companion to the villainous Dick Dastardly. Muttley is loyal to Dastardly, but his motivations are primarily driven by self-interest and the promise of rewards, often in the form of medals or treats.

Muttley's mischievous nature is showcased through his participation in the zany races. While Dastardly concocts elaborate schemes to win, Muttley often finds himself caught up in the chaos and hilarity that ensues. Despite his attempts to cheat and sabotage, Muttley's schemes are usually foiled, leading to comedic outcomes.

Though Muttley may be driven by self-interest, he does have moments of genuine compassion and camaraderie. On occasion, he showcases loyalty and teamwork, particularly when working alongside his fellow racers. Muttley's soft spot for his racing companions is revealed, making him a more complex and relatable character.

Muttley's distinct wheezy laugh has become an iconic part of his character. It adds a touch of humor and mischief to his actions, making him instantly recognizable and memorable among fans of the series.

Muttley's portrayal in "Wacky Races" exemplifies the timeless archetype of the lovable yet cunning sidekick. His mischievous antics and iconic laugh have made him a beloved character in the realm of animated television, leaving a lasting impression on audiences who appreciate his sneaky charm and comedic value.

Nana

Nana is a character from J.M. Barrie's classic story "Peter Pan" and its various adaptations, including the beloved Disney animated film. Nana is a lovable and nurturing St. Bernard dog who serves as the caretaker of the Darling children.

Nana's physical appearance is that of a large and gentle St. Bernard, characterized by her droopy jowls, warm eyes, and a wagging tail that expresses her affectionate nature. She is often seen wearing a nurse's hat, symbolizing her role as the nurturing guardian of the Darling children.

Nana's character is depicted as loving, protective, and incredibly devoted to the Darling family. She serves as both a guardian and a friend, watching over Wendy, John, and Michael with unwavering dedication. Nana's maternal instincts shine through as she ensures their safety and well-being, making her an integral part of the family dynamic.

Nana's interactions with the children bring moments of comfort, warmth, and playfulness. She engages in playful antics, such as playing with a ball or pretending to be a nurse, creating a sense of joy and light-heartedness in the household. Nana's presence offers a sense of stability and security to the Darling children, reinforcing the theme of the importance of familial bonds.

Nana's character is portrayed as intelligent and perceptive, often noticing and responding to events before others do. She exhibits a sense of intuition and understands the needs of the children, providing a calming and reassuring presence during times of fear or uncertainty.

Nana's portrayal in "Peter Pan" highlights the unconditional love and loyalty that dogs can offer. Her role extends beyond that of a pet, symbolizing the nurturing and protective qualities found within the animal-human bond. Nana represents the embodiment of trust, care, and comfort, reminding both the characters and the audience of the importance of these qualities in navigating the adventures and challenges of life.

Odie

Odie is a character from the popular comic strip and animated series "Garfield." Odie is a lovable and energetic beagle who serves as the faithful and endearing companion to the titular character, Garfield the cat.

Odie's physical appearance is that of a medium-sized beagle with floppy ears, a wagging tail, and a perpetually happy expression. He is portrayed as an adorable and playful dog, often seen with his tongue hanging out, showcasing his exuberance and enthusiasm.

Odie's character is known for his boundless energy, innocence, and unwavering loyalty. He is depicted as a lovable goofball, always eager to please and make others happy. Odie's friendly and trusting nature often makes him an easy target for Garfield's playful pranks and schemes.

Despite being the subject of Garfield's tricks, Odie's character embodies forgiveness and a genuine desire for companionship. He adores Garfield and seeks his approval, even if it means enduring the occasional playful teasing. Odie's unconditional love and loyalty serve as a reminder of the pure and genuine bond between a dog and its owner.

Odie's physical comedy and animated expressions add to his charm and appeal. His playful antics, such as chasing his tail or enthusiastically fetching objects, bring lightheartedness and humor to the comic strip and animated series. Odie's presence often serves as a catalyst for laughter and entertainment, making him a fan favorite.

Although Odie is not known for his intelligence, his innocent nature and good heartedness make him endearing to both the characters in the strip and the readers or viewers. He brings an element of joy and innocence to the Garfield universe, creating a balance with the cynical and lazy Garfield.

Old Yeller

"Old Yeller" was written by Fred Gipson, an American author known for his contributions to children's literature. Fred Gipson was born in 1908 in Texas, and he drew inspiration from his own experiences growing up in the rugged Texas countryside.

Gipson's storytelling ability shines through in "Old Yeller," as he masterfully captures the essence of frontier life and the deep bond between humans and animals. Through his vivid descriptions and heartfelt narrative, Gipson creates a compelling tale that resonates with readers of all ages.

"Old Yeller" was published in 1956 and quickly became a beloved classic. Gipson's portrayal of the bond between a boy and his loyal dog struck a chord with audiences, showcasing his ability to evoke deep emotions through his writing. The book's success led to the adaptation of "Old Yeller" into a popular film in 1957, further solidifying its status as a treasured piece of literature.

Old Yeller is a loyal and courageous mixed-breed dog who becomes a beloved member of the Coates family and plays a central role in their lives.

Old Yeller's physical appearance is that of a rugged and sturdy dog, with a yellow or golden coat, hence his name. He possesses a strong and noble demeanor, with alert eyes and a confident stance that reflects his resilience and determination.

Old Yeller's character is defined by his unwavering loyalty, bravery, and protective instincts. He proves himself to be an exceptional and invaluable companion to the Coates family, always ready to defend them from danger and provide unwavering support during challenging times.

Old Yeller's journey begins as a stray dog who befriends Travis, the young protagonist of the story. As the narrative unfolds, Old Yeller's presence becomes increasingly vital to the family's survival in the harsh wilderness of Texas. He proves his worth by protecting the family from various threats, including dangerous animals and hostile situations.

Despite his tough exterior, Old Yeller also displays a gentle and affectionate side. He forms a deep bond with Travis and his younger brother, Arliss, serving as their trusted and devoted friend. Old Yeller's nurturing nature is particularly evident in his interactions with Arliss, where he acts as a guardian and playmate.

Old Yeller's character is tested when he contracts rabies while defending the family from a rabid wolf. In a heartbreaking climax, Travis is forced to make a difficult decision, demonstrating the theme of sacrifice and the harsh realities of life in the frontier.

Otis

Otis is a character from the film "The Adventures of Milo and Otis." He is an energetic and curious pug who embarks on various adventures alongside his best friend, Milo the orange tabby cat.

Otis' physical appearance is characterized by his squished face, wrinkled forehead, and round, bulging eyes that add to his endearing charm. He has a stocky build and a wagging tail that reflects his enthusiasm and playful nature.

Otis' character is defined by his infectious joy and boundless energy. He approaches life with an optimistic and carefree attitude, always ready for the next adventure. His mischievous and adventurous spirit often leads him and Milo into exciting and sometimes perilous situations.

Despite his sometimes-impulsive nature, Otis is portrayed as a loyal and reliable friend. He exhibits a strong bond with Milo, often serving as the voice of reason and providing reassurance during their escapades. Otis' steadfast loyalty and protective instincts make him a trusted companion and a source of comfort for Milo.

Otis' playful antics and humorous interactions with Milo create moments of levity and warmth throughout the film. He engages in entertaining activities such as chasing butterflies, rolling in the grass, and playfully teasing Milo, showcasing his playful nature and adding to the film's sense of fun.

Underneath his playful exterior, Otis also displays moments of vulnerability and emotional depth. His character demonstrates empathy and compassion, especially when Milo encounters challenges or dangers. Otis supports his friend unconditionally, reminding audiences of the power of friendship and camaraderie.

Perdita

Perdita is a character from the animated film "101 Dalmatians" based on the classic novel by Dodie Smith. She is a beautiful and loving Dalmatian who plays a vital role in the heartwarming tale of courage, family, and adventure.

Perdita's physical appearance is characterized by her sleek white coat adorned with distinctive black spots. She has kind and expressive eyes that reflect her nurturing and gentle nature. Perdita possesses an elegant and graceful demeanor, further enhancing her beauty and charm.

Perdita's character is portrayed as loving, caring, and fiercely protective. She is the mate of Pongo, another Dalmatian, and together they form a devoted and inseparable pair. Perdita's maternal instincts shine through when she becomes a mother to a litter of adorable Dalmatian puppies, including the mischievous and courageous protagonist, Patch.

Perdita's unwavering love and dedication are evident in her willingness to go to great lengths to protect her family. When her puppies are stolen by the villainous Cruella de Vil, Perdita showcases incredible bravery and resourcefulness as she joins forces with other animal companions to rescue her beloved pups.

Throughout the film, Perdita demonstrates strength, resilience, and a deep sense of loyalty. She acts as a guiding force for her puppies, teaching them valuable lessons about family, unity, and the importance of staying true to oneself.

Perdita's character stands out for her kindness and gentle nature. She is known for her nurturing qualities, not only for her own puppies but also for other animals in need. Perdita's motherly instincts extend beyond her immediate family, showcasing her capacity for love and compassion.

In addition to her role as a mother, Perdita also embodies the spirit of adventure and perseverance. She braves numerous obstacles, displaying determination and courage while navigating the treacherous journey to rescue her puppies from Cruella de Vil's clutches.

Perdita's portrayal in "101 Dalmatians" captures the timeless bond between a mother and her offspring. Her character exemplifies the qualities of love, sacrifice, and the strength that comes from the unity of a family. Perdita's presence adds warmth, heart, and a sense of hope to the narrative, making her a beloved and integral part of the story.

Pete the Pup (aka Petey)

Pete the Pup, also known as Petey, is an iconic character from the "Our Gang" (aka "The Little Rascals") series of comedic short films. He is an American Pit Bull Terrier with distinct markings that make him easily recognizable.

Pete's physical appearance is characterized by a predominantly white coat with a ring around one eye and a spot over the other, giving him a unique and endearing look. These markings, often referred to as an "eye patch" or "target mark," contribute to his iconic and memorable appearance.

Pete's character is known for his gentle nature, intelligence, and unwavering loyalty. He is portrayed as a lovable and friendly dog, always ready to be a part of the gang's adventures and provide companionship for the children.

Pete's interactions with the other characters highlight his playful and mischievous side. He often participates in the gang's comedic escapades, adding an element of humor and lightheartedness to their antics. Pete's presence brings joy and laughter to the group, and his expressive eyes and wagging tail reflect his enthusiasm and excitement.

Beyond his playful demeanor, Pete is depicted as a steadfast and reliable companion. He forms strong bonds with the children and is often seen by their side, offering support, comfort, and protection. Pete's loyalty is unwavering, and he serves as a symbol of the enduring friendship and trust that can exist between humans and animals.

Pongo

Pongo is a central character in the animated film "101 Dalmatians" based on the classic novel by Dodie Smith. He is a courageous and caring Dalmatian who is owned by the human character named Roger.

Pongo's physical appearance is marked by his sleek and elegant white coat covered in distinctive black spots. He has a strong and noble stance, reflecting his protective nature and his role as the leader of his Dalmatian family.

Pongo's character is characterized by his intelligence, loyalty, and unwavering love for his family. As Roger's loyal companion, Pongo demonstrates his intelligence and resourcefulness throughout the film, often aiding Roger in his creative endeavors.

As a father, Pongo is devoted to his mate, Perdita, and their relationship serves as a strong foundation for their family. Pongo's love for Perdita is evident in his actions and his desire to protect and provide for her and their puppies. He is a caring and nurturing father figure to his lively and mischievous litter of Dalmatian puppies, particularly forming a special bond with his son, Patch.

Pongo's bravery and determination become apparent when his puppies are kidnapped by the villainous Cruella de Vil. He takes charge, leading a daring rescue mission to bring his family back together. Pongo's leadership skills and unwavering commitment to his loved ones inspire the other dogs in the film, emphasizing the importance of family, unity, and standing up against injustice.

Despite the challenges and dangers they face, Pongo maintains a calm and composed demeanor. He embodies the virtues of patience, bravery, and selflessness, showcasing his dedication to his family and his unwavering sense of responsibility.

Poochie

Poochie is a fictional character within "The Itchy & Scratchy Show," a cartoon series featured in the animated TV show, The Simpsons. Poochie is a hip and radical cartoon dog created as a desperate attempt to inject new life into the declining ratings of the show.

Poochie's physical appearance embodies the stereotypical characteristics of a cool and edgy cartoon character. He has a sleek and stylish design with a colorful and eye-catching outfit, including sunglasses, a leather jacket, and trendy accessories. Poochie's appearance is meant to exude an aura of contemporary pop culture and appeal to the younger audience.

Poochie is depicted as energetic, enthusiastic, and always ready for an adventure. He speaks in a distinctive and exaggerated manner, using slang and catchphrases that were popular at the time of his creation. Poochie's dialogue often includes references to popular culture, reflecting the attempt to make him relatable and "hip" to the audience.

Despite his attempts to be the epitome of coolness, Poochie's character is often met with mixed reactions. Some viewers find him entertaining and refreshing, while others see him as an obvious marketing gimmick and a shallow addition to the show. This divide in opinion adds an element of humor and self-awareness to the character.

Poochie's role within "The Itchy & Scratchy Show" is to inject excitement and novelty into the established formula of the series. He is often involved in action-packed sequences and thrilling scenarios, showcasing his "extreme" and daredevil nature.

Porkchop

Porkchop is a beloved canine character from the animated TV series "Disney's Doug." He serves as the loyal and supportive best friend of the show's protagonist, Doug Funnie.

Physically, Porkchop is an anthropomorphic and clever-looking Bull Terrier with a white coat and expressive dark eyes. He has a unique personality and charm that make him instantly recognizable and endearing to viewers.

Porkchop's character is defined by his intelligence, resourcefulness, and unwavering loyalty to Doug. Despite being a dog, Porkchop often displays a remarkable level of understanding and communication, seemingly grasping the complexities of human interactions.

Porkchop is not just a loyal companion, but he is also Doug's trusted confidant. He listens attentively to Doug's problems and provides silent support and comfort when needed. Porkchop's empathetic nature makes him an ideal companion for Doug, always there to offer a paw or a sympathetic gaze during challenging moments.

One of Porkchop's standout qualities is his cleverness and ability to navigate various situations. He often assists Doug in finding creative solutions to problems, demonstrating an astute and quick-thinking nature. Whether it's helping Doug come up with an idea for a school project or aiding him in navigating social dilemmas, Porkchop proves to be an invaluable friend.

Porthos

Porthos is a delightful Beagle and beloved pet of Captain Jonathan Archer in the television series "Star Trek: Enterprise." As a faithful and ever-loyal companion to Captain Archer, Porthos adds a touch of warmth and charm to the crew of the Enterprise.

Porthos is an adorable Beagle with a tri-color coat of brown, black, and white markings. His expressive eyes and wagging tail reflect his friendly and affectionate nature. Porthos often sports a tiny Starfleet uniform tailored specifically for him, symbolizing his honorary membership within the crew.

Porthos' character is defined by his unwavering loyalty and companionship. He is always by Captain Archer's side, offering comfort, support, and a friendly presence during the challenges of deep space exploration. Porthos serves as a reminder of the importance of companionship and the bonds that can form between humans and their pets.

Although Porthos cannot communicate in the same way as his human counterparts, his presence has a profound impact on the crew. He brings a sense of normalcy and humanity to the starship, reminding everyone of the comforts of home and the joys of simple pleasures. Porthos' playful antics and enthusiasm inject moments of levity into the intense and often dangerous missions undertaken by the crew.

Porthos' role extends beyond being a cherished pet; he also serves as a confidant and source of comfort for Captain Archer. As the captain faces the burdens of command, Porthos offers a sympathetic ear and unconditional love. Porthos' ability to provide solace during trying times highlights the profound emotional connection that can exist between humans and their animal companions.

Porthos' presence in "Star Trek: Enterprise" reflects the show's commitment to exploring the human experience in the vastness of space. He serves as a reminder of the importance of compassion, companionship, and the shared connection between different species. Porthos' inclusion in the series showcases the belief that even in the future, the bond between a human and their pet remains a source of comfort and joy.

Porthos' endearing character, loyalty, and loving presence make him a fan-favorite in the "Star Trek" franchise. His inclusion in the series reinforces the notion that our furry friends can play a vital role in our lives, even in the farthest reaches of the galaxy.

Precious Pup

Precious Pupp is a delightful, animated character from "The Atom Ant/Secret Squirrel Show" who captures hearts with his small stature, boundless courage, and knack for finding himself in hilarious situations. As a pint-sized but incredibly brave canine, Precious Pupp embodies the classic underdog archetype. With his round, expressive eyes, and wagging tail, he exudes an irresistible charm that endears him to viewers of all ages.

Precious Pupp's adventures often revolve around comical misunderstandings and mishaps, showcasing his innocent nature and playful spirit. Despite his size, he fearlessly faces challenges, whether it's thwarting the plans of villains or protecting his loved ones. Precious Pupp's loyalty knows no bounds, especially when it comes to his owner, Granny Sweet. He goes to great lengths to keep her safe, often with hilarious and unexpected outcomes. His small size and the resulting physical comedy make him a constant source of laughter in the show.

Beneath his playful exterior, Precious Pupp has a heart of gold. He exemplifies unwavering loyalty and determination, never hesitating to step up and do what's right. Precious Pupp's endearing personality and ability to make viewers laugh through his misadventures make him a memorable character in "The Atom Ant/Secret Squirrel Show." He reminds us that even the smallest of heroes can have a big impact and that laughter is never far behind in the most unexpected situations.

Red Dog

Red Dog is a remarkable and legendary canine character from the film "Red Dog." Based on a true story, Red Dog captivates audiences with his endearing personality and unwavering loyalty.

Physically, Red Dog is a robust and handsome, red-colored Kelpie breed with a striking coat that matches his name. His expressive eyes and friendly smile reflect his gentle nature and charismatic charm, making him instantly captivating.

Red Dog's character is characterized by his remarkable intelligence, independence, and devotion. He roams the Australian outback, captivating the hearts of the local community and forging deep connections with people he encounters along his journey.

Red Dog becomes a beloved figure in the small mining town of Dampier, where he forms a special bond with the residents. Despite being a stray, Red Dog embraces his role as a friend and confidant, bringing joy and solace to those he encounters. He listens to their worries, offers companionship, and serves as a reminder of the loyalty and love that dogs can provide.

Red Dog's loyalty and dedication are most evident in his unwavering commitment to his master, John. Red Dog embarks on a heartfelt quest to find John, displaying remarkable determination and an intuitive understanding of human connections. His journey becomes a testament to the enduring bond between humans and dogs and showcases the lengths a loyal companion will go to reunite with their beloved owner.

Beyond his loyalty, Red Dog's mischievous and playful nature adds a delightful sense of humor to the story. His antics and adventures in the outback, often portrayed with a touch of charm and cleverness, bring a sense of joy and lightness to the film.

Red Dog's character represents the profound impact that a dog can have on a community and the power of their unwavering loyalty and love. His story showcases the importance of connection, compassion, and the enduring bonds that can be formed with our furry friends.

Ren

Ren Höek is a main character in the iconic TV cartoon series "Ren & Stimpy." Ren is a short-tempered, neurotic, and often unhinged Chihuahua with a complex personality that makes him both endearing and unpredictable.

Physically, Ren is a small, wiry Chihuahua with a light tan coat, large ears, and bulging eyes that reflect his constant state of agitation. His facial expressions and body language perfectly convey his range of emotions, from anger and frustration to moments of vulnerability and insecurity.

Ren's character is defined by his explosive and erratic behavior, often displaying intense mood swings that lead him into all sorts of outrageous situations. He is known for his short fuse and has a tendency to overreact to the simplest of provocations, which leads to comedic and chaotic outcomes.

Despite his volatile nature, Ren is fiercely loyal to his dim-witted but lovable friend Stimpy. Their dynamic as an odd couple creates the foundation for the show's humor and hijinks. Ren often finds himself as the more rational and exasperated half of the duo, trying to keep Stimpy's carefree and naive nature in check.

Beneath his volatile exterior, Ren's character exhibits moments of vulnerability and self-doubt, highlighting his complex and multifaceted nature. He wrestles with his own insecurities and frequently battles his own inner demons, contributing to his unpredictable behavior.

Ren's unique voice, provided by the show's creator John Kricfalusi, adds to the distinctiveness of his character. His exaggerated mannerisms, expressive voice, and sharp wit make him a memorable and iconic figure in the world of animated television.

Ren Höek's portrayal in "Ren & Stimpy" showcases the show's irreverent and offbeat sense of humor, pushing the boundaries of animation and delivering entertainment that appeals to both children and adults. Ren's complex personality, marked by his explosive nature, vulnerabilities, and loyalty, makes him a captivating and beloved character in the world of cartoons.

Ribsy

Ribsy is a lovable and mischievous dog character in the children's book "Ribsy" written by Beverly Cleary. With his spirited personality and knack for getting into hilarious predicaments, Ribsy captivates readers of all ages.

Physically, Ribsy is a scruffy mixed-breed dog with a shaggy coat, floppy ears, and an endearing face. His brown fur and wagging tail give him an approachable and friendly appearance that immediately draws people to him.

Ribsy's character is characterized by his adventurous spirit and boundless curiosity. He often finds himself caught up in humorous and sometimes chaotic situations, whether it's chasing after a delicious hamburger or accidentally boarding the wrong bus.

Despite his occasional misadventures, Ribsy is known for his unwavering loyalty and love for his human companion, Henry Huggins. Ribsy's bond with Henry forms the heart of the story, showcasing the deep connection between a boy and his dog.

Ribsy's mischievous antics and amusing escapades bring joy and laughter to both the characters within the book and readers. From his interactions with other neighborhood dogs to his encounters with various people and places, Ribsy's adventures offer a delightful and entertaining reading experience.

Beverly Cleary's vivid descriptions and engaging storytelling bring Ribsy to life, making him a relatable and memorable character. Through Ribsy's perspective, readers gain insight into the world of a lovable, furry companion who navigates the challenges and joys of everyday life.

Rin Tin Tin

Rin Tin Tin is a fictional canine character who has captivated audiences for decades with his exceptional bravery, intelligence, and loyalty. He is a striking German Shepherd, possessing a regal and commanding presence. Rin Tin Tin stands tall at the shoulder, his muscular build conveying strength and agility. His coat is thick, glossy, and adorned with a combination of golden and black fur, enhancing his noble appearance. With sharp, intelligent eyes that radiate understanding and a keen awareness, Rin Tin Tin captivates all who behold him.

Character Sketch: Rin Tin Tin embodies the epitome of heroism and devotion. His character is characterized by unwavering loyalty, unparalleled bravery, and exceptional intelligence. He serves as a protector and guardian, always ready to put himself in harm's way to ensure the safety of those he holds dear. Rin Tin Tin's unwavering sense of duty and his commitment to justice make him a symbol of hope and inspiration.

Rin Tin Tin's origins can be traced back to the early 1920s when he made his first appearance on the silver screen. The character of Rin Tin Tin was created by Lee Duncan, an American soldier who found a litter of German Shepherd puppies in France during World War I. Duncan rescued one of the puppies and named him Rin Tin Tin after a good luck charm he found in a bombed-out French kennel. After the war, Duncan brought Rin Tin Tin back to the United States and trained him for film and television.

Rin Tin Tin's journey to stardom began with a fortunate opportunity in the film industry. It all started when a camera-shy wolf was unable to perform for the movie "The Man from Hell's River" (1922), starring Wallace Beery. Sensing an opportunity, Rin Tin Tin, guided by the voice commands of his owner, Lee Duncan, stepped in as a replacement. His exceptional obedience and ease of work impressed the director, and the dog's performance saved the day. The film was completed with Rin Tin Tin, although he was initially billed as "Rin Tan."

Due to Rin Tin Tin's remarkable training and reliability, he frequently found himself cast in roles as a wolf or wolf-hybrid throughout his career. Filmmakers found it much more convenient to work with a trained dog rather than an unpredictable wild animal. In another film in 1922 titled "My Dad," Rin Tin Tin played a small part as a household dog, and his credits proudly stated: "Rin Tin Tin – Played by himself."

Rin Tin Tin's big break arrived when he secured his first starring role in "Where the North Begins" (1923), alongside the popular silent screen actress Claire Adams. This film proved to be a resounding success, and its triumph is often credited with saving Warner Bros. from bankruptcy. Following this achievement, Rin Tin Tin went on to appear in 24 more films, each one enjoying significant popularity. The tremendous profits these films generated for Warner Bros. led to Rin Tin Tin being affectionately referred to as "the mortgage lifter" by insiders within the studio.

It is worth noting that a young screenwriter named Darryl F. Zanuck played a role in crafting stories for Rin Tin Tin. The tremendous success of the films featuring Rin Tin Tin propelled Zanuck to become a notable film producer, a testament to the impact and profitability associated with the charismatic canine star.

Overall, Rin Tin Tin's journey from replacing a camera-shy wolf to becoming a beloved and iconic film star was a remarkable one. His talents, obedience, and on-screen presence saved the day and contributed to the success of numerous films, securing his place in cinematic history. The influence of Rin Tin Tin's career extended beyond his own fame, elevating the careers of those involved in his productions and leaving an indelible mark on the film industry.

Rowlf

Rowlf the Dog is a beloved character from "The Muppets" TV show and franchise. He is a lovable and talented puppet dog with a distinctive appearance and a charming demeanor. Rowlf stands at a medium height among the Muppets, with shaggy fur that is predominantly brown, giving him a warm and inviting look. His expressive eyes twinkle with a mix of intelligence and playfulness, making him instantly endearing to both his fellow Muppets and audiences.

Character Sketch: Rowlf the Dog is a multi-talented and charismatic character within "The Muppets" universe. Known for his musical abilities, Rowlf often showcases his skills as a pianist, captivating audiences with his delightful melodies and charming stage presence. His musical prowess extends to various genres, ranging from classical to jazz, allowing him to adapt to different styles and moods effortlessly.

Beyond his musical talents, Rowlf possesses a gentle and kind-hearted nature. He serves as a voice of reason and a trusted confidant among the Muppets, often offering wise and thoughtful advice to his friends. Rowlf's calm and level-headed approach to situations brings a sense of stability and harmony to the colorful chaos that often surrounds the Muppets.

Despite his composed demeanor, Rowlf has a mischievous side and a great sense of humor. He delights in engaging in playful banter and witty remarks, adding a touch of levity to any situation. Rowlf's comedic timing and clever one-liners make him a favorite among both the Muppets and viewers, consistently bringing laughter and joy to the screen.

Ruffles

Ruffles is an adorable and spirited dog who takes center stage in the heartwarming film "Hotel for Dogs." He is a small to medium-sized mixed breed with a charming and expressive face that reflects his playful and mischievous nature. Ruffles' fur is a fluffy combination of caramel and white, adding to his endearing appearance. His bright, alert eyes exude curiosity and intelligence, capturing the attention and affection of both the characters in the film and the audience.

Ruffles is a lovable and resourceful character in "Hotel for Dogs," known for his adventurous spirit and unwavering loyalty. Despite facing various challenges, Ruffles approaches life with a playful and optimistic attitude. He is always ready for new experiences and is not afraid to take risks in pursuit of creating a better life for himself and his fellow canine friends.

Ruffles is the epitome of a loyal companion, fiercely devoted to his human counterparts and fellow four-legged friends. His unwavering dedication and protective nature make him an invaluable member of the "Hotel for Dogs" community. Ruffles constantly looks out for the well-being of others, going to great lengths to ensure their safety and happiness.

With his clever and creative problem-solving skills, Ruffles becomes a leader within the makeshift hotel for dogs. He is quick on his paws and always finds innovative ways to improve their living situation, bringing a sense of comfort and stability to their lives. Ruffles' determination and resourcefulness inspire the other dogs to overcome obstacles and embrace their own potential.

Sam

Sam, a loyal and courageous German Shepherd, plays a pivotal role in the thrilling film "I Am Legend" alongside actor Will Smith. She is a strong and majestic canine, exhibiting the characteristics of her breed. Sam's sleek coat is a rich tan color, complementing her alert and intelligent brown eyes. With an athletic physique and a regal presence, she commands attention and embodies the resilience required to survive in a post-apocalyptic world.

Sam is more than just a companion to the protagonist in "I Am Legend." She serves as a symbol of unwavering loyalty, unwavering love, and a constant source of support amidst the desolation of a world ravaged by a devastating virus. Sam's bond with Will Smith's character, Robert Neville, is profound, representing the connection between humans and animals in the face of unimaginable circumstances.

Despite the challenges they face, Sam's unwavering loyalty and protective instincts shine through. She stands by Robert's side as a steadfast companion, providing comfort and companionship in a world where few survive. Sam's presence serves as a beacon of hope and a reminder of the enduring bond between humans and their animal counterparts.

Sam's intelligence and agility make her an invaluable ally in their struggle for survival. She navigates the decimated landscape with grace and assists Robert in his daily routines, ensuring their safety and well-being. Sam's keen senses and ability to detect danger contribute to their survival, making her an essential partner in their battle against the infected creatures that roam the city.

Beyond her protective nature, Sam brings moments of joy and levity to the film. Her playful spirit and affectionate gestures offer moments of respite from the bleakness of their surroundings. Sam's ability to find solace and happiness in the simplest of moments serves as a reminder of the resilience and adaptability of animals in the face of adversity.

Sam's character symbolizes the enduring bond between humans and their faithful companions. Her unwavering loyalty and devotion to Robert embody the unconditional love that dogs can provide, even in the darkest of times. Sam's presence in "I Am Legend" exemplifies the power of companionship and the indomitable spirit that can emerge from the depths of despair.

Sam Sheepdog

Sam Sheepdog is a beloved character from the Looney Tunes animated short films, known for his unwavering patience, strong work ethic, and his constant interactions with his counterpart, Ralph Wolf. As a sheepdog, Sam's primary duty is to guard the flock of sheep under his care, and he takes his job very seriously.

Sam is portrayed as a diligent and hardworking sheepdog, always alert and ready to protect the sheep from any harm. He is seen as a symbol of reliability and responsibility, faithfully carrying out his duties day after day. Despite the mischievous efforts of Ralph Wolf to outsmart him, Sam remains composed and determined, often matching wits with his adversary.

One of the endearing qualities of Sam Sheepdog is his unwavering commitment to his job and the sheep. He showcases incredible patience and a calm demeanor, even in the face of Ralph Wolf's relentless schemes. Sam's interactions with Ralph Wolf create a dynamic that is both comical and heartwarming, as they engage in a continuous battle of wits.

Sandy

Sandy is a lovable and faithful companion in the musical "Annie." He is a mixed-breed dog with sandy-colored fur, which perfectly matches his name. Sandy is Annie's loyal canine friend, and their bond is a heartwarming aspect of the story.

Character Sketch: Sandy is depicted as a scruffy and friendly dog with an endearing personality. Despite his rough appearance, his warm and gentle nature shines through. Sandy possesses a keen sense of loyalty and is deeply devoted to Annie, always staying by her side through thick and thin.
Sandy's expressions and body language often reflect his emotions, making him a delightful character to watch on stage. His expressive eyes and wagging tail communicate his joy and excitement, while his lowered head and droopy ears show his understanding and empathy during more poignant moments.

Sandy's role in the story goes beyond being Annie's pet. He serves as a symbol of hope, companionship, and unconditional love. Whether it's providing comfort during difficult times or adding a touch of comic relief, Sandy's presence brings joy and warmth to both the characters and the audience.
With his playful antics and unwavering loyalty, Sandy captures the hearts of the audience, becoming an integral part of the musical's charm. He represents the unwavering support that Annie finds in her journey, reminding everyone that even in the toughest of circumstances, love and loyalty can bring solace and strength.

One memorable moment in the musical "Annie" is when Sandy helps Annie escape from the orphanage. In a pivotal scene, Annie decides to run away after Miss Hannigan, the strict orphanage supervisor, mistreats her and her friends. With the help of a note, she had received from a mysterious benefactor, Annie realizes that her parents might be alive.

As Annie makes her daring escape, she sneaks out of the orphanage under the cover of darkness. Just as she is about to exit the gates, Sandy comes to her rescue. Sensing Annie's distress, Sandy manages to slip past the guards and join her on her adventure. With his keen sense of loyalty and determination, Sandy becomes her faithful companion on the journey to find her parents.

This moment not only showcases Sandy's intelligence and resourcefulness but also highlights the deep bond between him and Annie. Sandy's courageous act adds an element of suspense and excitement to the story, demonstrating that he is not just an ordinary pet but a true friend willing to risk it all for the ones he loves.

Santa's Little Helper (aka No. 8)

Santa's Little Helper, also known as No. 8, is a beloved fictional dog from the animated TV series "The Simpsons." He is an adorable and mischievous greyhound who plays a significant role in the Simpson family's life. No. 8 initially enters the scene as an abandoned racing dog, but his introduction leads to heartwarming and humorous adventures throughout the show.

No. 8, or Santa's Little Helper, is a lovable and energetic greyhound with sleek grey fur and expressive eyes. He exudes an aura of enthusiasm and curiosity, always ready to embark on new adventures. Despite being initially dismissed as a racing reject, No. 8 proves himself to be a cherished member of the Simpson family.

No. 8 has a playful and sometimes mischievous nature, which often lands him in comical situations. His antics range from chasing squirrels to knocking over household objects, bringing both chaos and laughter into the lives of the Simpson family. However, underneath his playful exterior, No. 8 possesses a heart full of love and loyalty.

No. 8's affectionate personality shines through in his interactions with the Simpsons. He adores Bart, the mischievous son of the family, and they share a special bond. No. 8 often joins Bart in his escapades, adding an extra layer of comedic charm to their adventures. He also displays great affection towards the other family members, providing comfort and support during their ups and downs.

Throughout the series, No. 8's presence brings joy and a sense of unity to the Simpson family. He teaches them important life lessons about love, loyalty, and the value of having a furry friend by their side. No. 8's endearing qualities make him not just a beloved animated character but also an iconic symbol of companionship and unconditional love in "The Simpsons."

Scooby-Doo & Family

Scooby-Doo is a legendary fictional dog from the animated television series "Scooby-Doo." He is a lovable and goofy K-9 who is both the namesake and the heart of the Mystery Inc. gang. Scooby-Doo's distinctive personality and his insatiable appetite for food contribute to his charm and make him a beloved character in popular culture.

Scooby-Doo is a large and affable Great Dane with a distinctive brown coat marked with black spots. His appearance, coupled with his endearing mannerisms, instantly make him an iconic and recognizable character. Scooby-Doo is often portrayed as a bit clumsy, but his actions are always driven by good intentions and a strong sense of loyalty to his friends.

Scooby-Doo's love for food is a defining trait and a constant source of humor in the series. He is known for his insatiable appetite, often devouring enormous amounts of food in record time. This voraciousness adds an element of comedy to the show and often leads to comical situations. Despite his comical antics, Scooby-Doo is incredibly brave when it comes to solving mysteries with his friends.

Despite his occasional cowardice, Scooby-Doo's loyalty to his friends and his desire to protect them are unwavering. He is often seen as the heart of the Mystery Inc. gang, supporting and encouraging his friends during their investigations. Scooby-Doo's courage shines through when faced with monsters and ghosts, and he often surprises everyone with his bravery in critical moments.

Scooby-Doo's cousin, Scooby-Dum, is an endearing and lovable character in the Scooby-Doo universe. He is a dim-witted but well-meaning Great Dane who brings his own unique charm to the Mystery Inc. gang. Similar in appearance to Scooby-Doo, with a light greyish blue coat, and a red hat and collar.

Scooby-Dum's well-meaning nature often leads him into humorous situations, as he tends to misinterpret or misunderstand clues and instructions. However, despite his lack of intelligence, Scooby-Dum has a heart of gold and possesses a strong sense of loyalty towards his cousin and the rest of the Mystery Inc. gang.

Scooby-Dum's appearance in the series often brings a dynamic shift to the group dynamics, injecting moments of comedy and creating opportunities for Scooby-Doo to showcase his intelligence in contrast. Despite his shortcomings, Scooby-Dum is always ready to lend a helping paw and joins in on the adventures with enthusiasm, even if he may not fully comprehend the situation.

Scrappy-Doo is Scooby-Doo's energetic and fearless nephew. Despite his small size, he compensates with his boldness and determination, often leading the group in solving mysteries.

Ruby-Doo is Scooby-Doo's sister. While she has not appeared in the animated series, she is mentioned in the Scooby-Doo and Scrappy-Doo comic book series, expanding the canine family's lineage.

Yabba-Doo is Scooby-Doo's cowboy cousin. He hails from the Wild West and occasionally joins the gang on their adventures, showcasing his cowboy skills and adding a touch of western flair to the mysteries.

Dooby-Doo is Scooby-Doo's brother who is known for being a disco dancer. Although he has not appeared in the animated series, he is mentioned in the Scooby-Doo and Scrappy-Doo comic book series, bringing a groovy twist to the family.

Skippy-Doo is Scooby-Doo's brother who is an inventor. Like Dooby-Doo, Skippy-Doo has not appeared in the animated series but is referenced in the Scooby-Doo and Scrappy-Doo comic book series. His inventive nature likely adds a unique perspective to problem-solving.

Scooter

Scooter is a lovable and mischievous character in the heartwarming Disney film "Pete's Dragon." He is a small, green dragon with a playful personality that instantly captures the audience's attention. Scooter is filled with childlike curiosity and wonder, always eager to explore his surroundings and interact with the people and creatures he encounters. With his large, expressive eyes and endearing charm, Scooter quickly becomes an integral part of the story, bringing joy and laughter to both the characters on-screen and the viewers.

Despite his small size, Scooter possesses incredible powers. He can breathe fire, albeit in small bursts, and can fly, albeit not as gracefully as the majestic dragons of legend. However, what truly sets Scooter apart is his kind heart. He is fiercely loyal to his newfound friend, Pete, a young boy who has lost his parents and found solace in the company of the magical dragon. Scooter's protective nature and unwavering support become a source of strength for Pete, as they embark on an extraordinary adventure together.

Scooter's innocence and pure-heartedness shine through every action and interaction. He has an infectious energy that brings out the best in those around him. Whether it's playfully chasing his tail or innocently exploring the world, Scooter reminds everyone of the beauty and magic that can be found in even the smallest of creatures. With his boundless enthusiasm and unwavering friendship, Scooter leaves a lasting impression on audiences and proves that true heroes come in all shapes and sizes.

Scud

Scud, the mischievous canine character from the animated film "Toy Story," is a force to be reckoned with. As Sid's loyal and energetic bull terrier, Scud embodies the quintessential antagonist, constantly causing havoc for the beloved toys. With his perpetually wagging tail and relentless determination, Scud is always on the hunt, sniffing out any toy that dares to cross his path. His intimidating appearance, coupled with his unwavering loyalty to Sid, makes him a formidable opponent for Woody, Buzz, and the rest of the toys.

Scud's actions are driven by his instinctive nature as a dog, making him a relentless pursuer of his toy prey. With his keen sense of smell and lightning-fast speed, he becomes a constant source of fear and tension for the toys, who must navigate Sid's room with utmost caution to avoid detection. Scud's bark is ferocious, and his sheer size and strength give him a menacing presence. Despite being a source of danger, Scud's portrayal also adds an element of excitement and suspense to the film, creating memorable moments of high-stakes adventure.

While Scud serves as an antagonist in "Toy Story," he also represents the unwavering loyalty and protectiveness that dogs are known for. He is fiercely devoted to Sid, who, in his own way, provides him with care and companionship. Scud's loyalty is a double-edged sword, as it drives him to relentlessly pursue the toys but also endears him to Sid. His character serves as a reminder that even the most antagonistic figures can have their own unique qualities and motivations, adding depth to the overall narrative of the film.

Shadow

Shadow, the wise and loyal golden retriever in the heartwarming film "Homeward Bound: The Incredible Journey," captures the hearts of viewers with his steadfast devotion and unwavering determination. With his dignified presence and graying fur, Shadow exudes wisdom and maturity beyond his years. He is the epitome of a faithful companion, always looking out for his human family and fellow animal companions, Chance, and Sassy. Shadow's character is defined by his unwavering loyalty and his deep sense of responsibility to protect and guide those he cares about.

Shadow's calm and composed demeanor serves as an anchor for the group, providing a sense of stability and reassurance in the face of adversity. His wisdom is evident in his decision-making, as he often thinks before acting and considers the well-being of the entire group. Shadow's strong moral compass and noble character make him a role model for both the other animals and the audience alike. His patience and resilience in the face of challenges become a source of inspiration and hope throughout their incredible journey.

Beneath Shadow's wise and composed exterior lies a gentle and compassionate soul. He is always ready to offer comfort and support, even in the most challenging of situations. Shadow's love and devotion to his human family, especially his young owner Peter, is profound and unwavering. His determination to return home and be reunited with his beloved humans becomes a driving force that keeps the group pushing forward. Shadow's character embodies the timeless bond between humans and animals, showcasing the power of love and loyalty in the face of adversity.

Slinky Dog

Slinky Dog, the loyal and affable character from the animated film "Toy Story," is an instant favorite with his charming personality and unique design. With his slinky body and friendly disposition, Slinky Dog becomes a trusted companion and confidant to Woody and the other toys. Slinky's character is defined by his unwavering loyalty and his unshakeable belief in the importance of friendship. He is always ready to lend a helping paw and offer words of encouragement, making him a beloved member of the toy gang.

Despite his limitations in mobility, Slinky Dog compensates with a can-do attitude and a resilient spirit. He is known for his signature slinky spring action, which he uses to his advantage in various situations, stretching himself to new heights and lengths to overcome obstacles. Slinky's good-natured humor and positive outlook on life uplift the spirits of those around him, injecting a sense of light-heartedness and camaraderie into the adventures of the toys. His unwavering dedication to his friends and his willingness to go the extra mile make Slinky Dog a cherished and integral part of the Toy Story franchise.

Snuffles (aka Snooper)

Snuffles, also known as "Snooper" in some episodes, is a delightful and indispensable character from the animated TV show "Quick Draw McGraw." As a small white dog, Snuffles serves as a loyal and astute companion to the show's main protagonist, Quick Draw McGraw, assisting him in solving mysteries and capturing villains.

Snuffles embodies the classic sidekick archetype, showcasing unwavering loyalty and a keen sense of observation. Despite his small stature, he proves to be an invaluable asset to Quick Draw McGraw, often noticing important clues and providing crucial assistance in their adventures. Snuffles' sharp instincts and intelligence make him an essential partner in crime-solving, complementing Quick Draw's efforts with his own unique skills.

With his endearing appearance and expressive eyes, Snuffles captures the hearts of viewers, delivering comedic relief and heartfelt moments throughout the show. His interactions with Quick Draw McGraw often involve humorous exchanges and playful banter, adding depth and charm to their partnership.

Snuffles' character exemplifies trust, dedication, and resourcefulness. Despite being a small dog, he fearlessly confronts challenges, demonstrating bravery in the face of danger. Snuffles' unwavering support for Quick Draw McGraw makes him a beloved character in the series, showcasing the importance of trust and teamwork in solving mysteries and overcoming obstacles.

Spike & Tyke (Tom and Jerry)

Spike and Tyke are beloved recurring characters from the timeless animated series "Tom and Jerry." Spike, a tough and lovable bulldog, serves as a protective father figure to his son, Tyke, in the tumultuous world they share with the mischievous cat, Tom. Their dynamic adds depth and heart to the series, showcasing the strength of family bonds and the importance of standing up for those we care about.

Spike, with his intimidating appearance and deep growling voice, embodies a tough exterior that masks a heart of gold. He is fiercely loyal and exhibits a strong sense of justice, often coming to Tyke's aid whenever Tom tries to cause trouble. Despite his tough demeanor, Spike also displays a gentle and nurturing side, caring deeply for his son's well-being, and teaching him valuable life lessons.

Tyke, the adorable and innocent pup, looks up to his father with admiration and trust. Although young and still learning about the world, Tyke possesses a sense of curiosity and a mischievous streak of his own. However, he is often sheltered from harm by Spike's watchful eye and unwavering protection.

The dynamic between Spike and Tyke showcases the love, support, and guidance that exists within a family. They demonstrate the importance of looking out for one another, standing up against adversaries, and teaching valuable life lessons. Whether it's teaching Tyke how to navigate the challenges presented by Tom or simply spending quality time together, Spike and Tyke's bond is heartwarming and a testament to the enduring power of family.

Spike (Rugrats)

Spike, the lovable and adventurous canine from the animated TV series "Rugrats," adds an extra dose of excitement and companionship to the lives of the adventurous toddlers. With his floppy ears and wagging tail, Spike is always ready to join in on the fun and embark on new adventures with Tommy, Chuckie, and the rest of the gang. Spike's character is defined by his unwavering loyalty and his ability to bring joy and laughter to those around him.

Despite being a dog, Spike often acts as a trusted confidant and protector to the Rugrats. His presence offers comfort and reassurance, as he fearlessly stands by their side through every obstacle and challenge they face. Spike's playful nature and energetic spirit make him the perfect companion for the curious toddlers, joining in their imaginative games and adding a sense of mischief and excitement to their everyday lives.

Spike's endearing qualities extend beyond his interactions with the Rugrats. He also serves as a source of comic relief, with his humorous antics and comedic timing providing laughter to both the characters and the audience. His expressive eyes and genuine affection for the toddlers make him an integral part of the Rugrats' extended family, showcasing the enduring bond between children and their furry friends. Spike's character embodies the spirit of adventure and friendship, reminding us of the joy that can be found in the simplest of moments and the unconditional love that our four-legged companions bring into our lives.

Snoopy

Snoopy, the beloved beagle created by the iconic cartoonist Charles Schulz, has left an indelible mark on the world of comics and animation. Schulz's imaginative vision and artistic talent brought Snoopy to life, endowing him with a whimsical charm and a timeless appeal. Snoopy's character, lovingly crafted by Schulz, embodies the spirit of adventure and imagination that resonates with readers and viewers of all ages.

In Charles Schulz's hands, Snoopy became more than just a dog; he became an emblem of joy, resilience, and the power of imagination. Schulz's ability to infuse Snoopy's expressions and actions with a range of human-like emotions made him relatable to audiences worldwide. The artist's attention to detail, from Snoopy's iconic doghouse to his signature dance moves, added depth and authenticity to the character, making Snoopy a beloved figure in the Peanuts universe.

Schulz's masterful storytelling allowed Snoopy to transcend the boundaries of the comic strip, taking readers and viewers on imaginative journeys filled with laughter, friendship, and a touch of nostalgia. Snoopy's endearing quirks and his enduring friendship with Charlie Brown were brought to life by Schulz's pen, creating a bond between character and audience that has stood the test of time. Thanks to Charles Schulz's creative genius, Snoopy has become an enduring symbol of hope, imagination, and the power of dreams, continuing to captivate new generations, and reminding us of the profound impact that one cartoonist can have on popular culture.

Snowball

Snowball, a captivating character from the animated TV series "Rick and Morty," undergoes a remarkable transformation from a family pet to a highly intelligent and power-hungry dog. Initially introduced as an ordinary pet, Snowball's journey takes an unexpected turn as he gains intelligence and strives to assert dominance over humans, challenging their perceived superiority.

As Snowball evolves into a highly intelligent being, he grapples with his newfound understanding of the world and questions the dynamics of power. Driven by a desire for equality and justice, Snowball adopts a more ambitious persona and seeks to liberate other animals from human control. Through his story arc, Snowball explores themes of oppression, rebellion, and the pursuit of freedom.

Snowball's transformation highlights the complexities of intelligence and the potential consequences of power in the wrong hands. His character challenges the notion of humans' assumed superiority over animals, sparking philosophical discussions and reflections on ethics and morality. Snowball's journey serves as a thought-provoking commentary on society's power dynamics and the consequences of unchecked ambition.

Despite his newfound intelligence and ambition, Snowball's character still retains elements of his initial charm and innocence as a family pet. This duality adds depth and complexity to his portrayal, reminding viewers of the multifaceted nature of identity and the potential for good and evil in all beings.

Snowball's character arc in "Rick and Morty" serves as a cautionary tale, exploring the consequences of unchecked power and the complexities of moral decision-making. His story prompts viewers to reflect on the implications of intelligence and the responsibilities that come with it, ultimately encouraging us to question our own relationships with power and authority.

Snowy

Snowy, the faithful and resourceful canine companion in the adventures of Tintin, was brought to life by the Belgian cartoonist Georges Remi, better known as Hergé. Hergé's creation of Snowy, or Milou as he is known in the original French version, added an endearing and often comical element to the iconic comic series. As Tintin's loyal sidekick, Snowy's character is defined by his unwavering loyalty and his penchant for getting into amusing predicaments.

Hergé's attention to detail and his ability to convey Snowy's thoughts and emotions through expressive illustrations make the character a true scene-stealer. Snowy's distinctive white fur and mischievous personality have become synonymous with the Tintin series, delighting readers and fans worldwide. From joining Tintin in his investigative pursuits to offering moments of comedic relief, Snowy's presence is a testament to Hergé's creative genius and his ability to create memorable characters that resonate with audiences.

The origin of Snowy as a character lies in Hergé's own love for dogs, particularly his pet terrier, Fox. Drawing inspiration from real-life companions, Hergé imbued Snowy with a mix of loyalty, curiosity, and occasional mischief. The character's evolution throughout the Tintin series showcases Hergé's skill in character development and storytelling. Snowy's endearing qualities and his unwavering dedication to Tintin make him an integral part of the adventures, capturing the hearts of readers and exemplifying the enduring bond between humans and their animal companions.

Spot

Spot is an endearing and iconic character from the "Fun with Dick and Jane" series of basal readers. Created as a lovable and relatable learning tool, Spot serves as a helpful companion for young readers, aiding them on their journey to develop essential reading skills. Spot's role in the series is to engage children and make the learning process enjoyable and accessible.

With his charming personality and adorable appearance, Spot captures the attention and imagination of young readers. Spot is often depicted as a friendly and curious dog, embarking on various adventures that incorporate basic vocabulary and simple sentence structures. Through Spot's stories, children are introduced to fundamental reading concepts, such as letter recognition, phonics, and basic sentence comprehension.

Spot's relatability and relatability make him a beloved character among young readers. He acts as a guide, encouraging children to follow along and actively participate in the reading experience. Spot's presence creates a safe and supportive environment for children to practice their reading skills, fostering confidence and enthusiasm in their journey towards literacy.

Spot's character highlights the joy and excitement that can be found in the process of learning to read. He embodies the idea that reading can be both fun and rewarding, inspiring children to develop a love for books and storytelling. Spot's positive and encouraging nature serves as a reminder that each step taken towards literacy is a valuable achievement.

Sprocket

Sprocket, the intelligent sheepdog from the TV series "Fraggle Rock," is a cherished character who adds a delightful and endearing element to the show's adventures. Owned by Doc, Sprocket serves as a bridge between the human world and the whimsical underground realm of the Fraggles, playing a key role in the interactions and escapades that unfold.

Sprocket is portrayed as a loyal and astute companion, always by Doc's side and ready for any new discovery or adventure. With his expressive eyes and wagging tail, Sprocket showcases a range of emotions that help convey his understanding and connection with the Fraggles. His intelligence is evident in his ability to navigate the challenges of both the human and Fraggle worlds, often acting as a mediator between the two.

Through his interactions with the Fraggles, Sprocket brings a sense of curiosity and wonder to the show. His presence creates a link between the human world above and the enchanting underground world of the Fraggles, allowing viewers to experience the magic and excitement from both perspectives. Sprocket's interactions with the Fraggles offer moments of comedy, warmth, and valuable life lessons.

Sprocket's character symbolizes the power of friendship and the ability to find common ground in unexpected places. Despite the differences in their worlds, Sprocket builds a genuine bond with the Fraggles, displaying the importance of acceptance, understanding, and embracing diversity. His loyalty to Doc and his willingness to explore new realms demonstrate the spirit of adventure and open-mindedness that can lead to remarkable experiences and friendships.

Stella

Stella, the lovable and wise canine protagonist from the heartwarming novel and film "A Dog's Purpose," captivates audiences with her unwavering loyalty and her ability to teach invaluable life lessons. Written by W. Bruce Cameron, Stella's character embodies the pure and unconditional love that dogs offer to their human companions. From her playful puppyhood to her role as a devoted service dog, Stella's journey showcases the incredible bond between humans and their furry friends.

Throughout the story, Stella serves as a guiding presence, offering comfort, support, and unwavering devotion to the humans whose lives she touches. Her intuitive nature and ability to sense and understand human emotions make her an invaluable companion. Stella's character highlights the profound impact that dogs have on our lives, as she becomes a beacon of hope, love, and resilience in the face of adversity.

W. Bruce Cameron's skillful storytelling allows Stella's voice to shine through, as readers and viewers are invited into her world of wagging tails and unconditional love. Stella's character reminds us of the power of empathy, forgiveness, and the capacity for growth and change. Her story is a testament to the profound impact that our four-legged friends have on our lives, and how they have the remarkable ability to teach us valuable lessons about compassion and the true meaning of loyalty.

Strongheart

Strongheart, also known as Etzel von Oeringen, was a pioneering canine star of the silent film era and a real-life hero in his own right. Strongheart's character, both on and off the screen, embodied strength, intelligence, and unwavering loyalty. As one of the first canine actors to achieve widespread fame, Strongheart's legacy continues to inspire and captivate audiences even today.

Etzel von Oeringen, the male German Shepherd behind the character, was bred by Robert Niedhardt of Quedlinburg, Germany, had a remarkable journey. Trained as a police dog in Berlin and serving in the German Red Cross during World War I, Etzel's owner fell into poverty after the war and couldn't provide for him. To ensure his well-being, the owner turned down larger offers and instead sent Etzel to a trusted friend who operated a reputable kennel in White Plains, New York. At the age of three, Etzel made his way to the United States for sale. His talents caught the eye of Laurence Trimble, a film director, known for his work with Jean, the Vitagraph Dog, America's first canine movie star. Recognizing Etzel's potential, Trimble persuaded Jane Murfin, a screenwriter for his films, to purchase the dog. The publicity department of First National Pictures, which released Etzel's first film, suggested renaming him Strongheart.

Tige

Tige, also known as Buster Brown's faithful companion, is a remarkable K-9 creation brought to life by the imaginative mind of Richard F. Outcault in the world of cartoons. With a sturdy build and expressive eyes filled with warmth and intelligence, Tige embodies the quintessential image of a loyal canine companion. His playful nature and unwavering loyalty make him an inseparable part of Buster Brown's cartoon adventures, providing both comic relief and heartwarming moments. Tige's mischievousness and ability to anticipate Buster's needs add a touch of lightheartedness to their animated escapades, while his unwavering dedication and moral compass guide Buster, a mischievous young cartoon character with a zest for life, towards making the right decisions. Tige's boundless energy and endearing personality make him a beloved member of the cartoon community, spreading joy and laughter wherever their animated world takes them. Through Tige, readers are reminded of the profound bond between humans and animals, and the immeasurable value of true friendship that transcends the realm of cartoons.

Tige, created by Richard F. Outcault, is a faithful companion to Buster Brown, a mischievous young cartoon character full of life and curiosity. Possessing a sturdy build and a coat of short, sleek hair, Tige's animated appearance captures the essence of a loyal canine. His eyes radiate intelligence and warmth, captivating all who encounter him on the pages of cartoons. Tige's playful spirit adds a touch of mischief to their animated adventures, but his loyalty knows no bounds. He fearlessly accompanies Buster, guiding him towards the right path and reminding him of the importance of making good choices in their cartoon world. Tige's presence brings joy and laughter wherever they go, endearing them to cartoon audiences and serving as a testament to the profound bond between humans and animals, even within the realm of animated storytelling. In the company of Tige, Buster Brown experiences the true meaning of friendship, showcasing the incredible value of companionship that resonates beyond the boundaries of the cartoon world. Together, Buster and Tige embark on countless animated escapades, creating enduring memories that entertain audiences and remind them of the power of friendship in both the animated realm and the real world.

Toby

Toby, the loyal and resourceful dog in Arthur Conan Doyle's novel "The Sign of the Four," serves as an asset in aiding Sherlock Holmes in his investigations. Owned by Mr. Sherman, Toby plays a significant role in unraveling the mysteries that Holmes encounters throughout the story.

Toby is portrayed as an intelligent and perceptive dog with a keen sense of smell and a knack for tracking scents. He becomes an invaluable ally to Sherlock Holmes, using his exceptional olfactory abilities to follow trails, locate missing objects, and uncover hidden clues. Toby's contribution to the investigative process highlights the remarkable skills that animals possess and their capacity to assist in solving complex cases.

Beyond his tracking abilities, Toby also demonstrates unwavering loyalty and affection towards his owner and Holmes. His presence adds a touch of warmth and companionship to the otherwise intense and challenging world of crime-solving. Toby's devotion and trust in his human companions underline the profound bond between animals and humans, reminding readers of the power of mutual trust and reliance.

Toby's character showcases the significance of paying attention to even the smallest details in an investigation. His role in "The Sign of the Four" exemplifies how different perspectives, including those of animals, can offer unique insights that aid in solving mysteries. Toby's inclusion in the story reminds us of the valuable contributions animals can make and the importance of appreciating their remarkable instincts.

Overall, Toby's presence in Arthur Conan Doyle's novel adds depth and intrigue to the narrative. His intelligence, loyalty, and exceptional tracking skills make him an essential partner to Sherlock Holmes.

Toto

Toto, the faithful canine companion in "The Wizard of Oz," is a small but spirited Cairn Terrier with a heart full of bravery. Despite his size, Toto proves to be an integral part of Dorothy's journey, serving as her loyal friend and protector throughout their adventures in the magical Land of Oz. Toto's unwavering loyalty and intuition make him an endearing character, capturing the hearts of audiences with his adorable presence and boundless courage.

One of the most memorable scenes featuring Toto occurs when Dorothy, played by Judy Garland, finds herself in the mysterious and vibrant Land of Oz. As she steps out of her sepia-toned, black-and-white world and into the vibrant technicolor surroundings, Toto's curiosity gets the better of him. He starts exploring the enchanting landscape, only to find himself face to face with the formidable Wicked Witch of the West. With a quick bark and a brave dash, Toto manages to escape the clutches of the wicked witch, evoking a sense of relief and admiration from viewers. This scene not only showcases Toto's mischievous nature but also highlights his role as Dorothy's protector, emphasizing the unbreakable bond between them.

Toto's character is portrayed as both mischievous and perceptive. He has a knack for getting into trouble, often finding himself amid curious situations. However, his keen senses and sharp instincts often lead him to uncover the truth and expose the facade of those they encounter. Toto's role extends beyond that of a mere pet; he becomes Dorothy's confidant and moral compass, guiding her towards the right path and offering comfort in times of uncertainty. With his unwavering devotion and unwavering spirit, Toto leaves an indelible mark on the hearts of viewers, reminding us of the extraordinary impact that even the smallest companions can have in our lives.

Tramp

Tramp, the charismatic and street-smart mutt in the animated film "Lady and the Tramp," is a charming rogue with a heart of gold. He roams the streets with confidence and a carefree attitude, surviving on his wits and street smarts. Tramp's scruffy appearance and roguish charm make him an instantly lovable character, capturing the hearts of audiences with his mischievous grin and playful nature.

One of the most iconic scenes featuring Tramp takes place during a romantic dinner at Tony's Italian restaurant. Lady, a refined and pampered Cocker Spaniel, finds herself in a challenging situation when she is chased by a pack of street dogs. Just when it seems like all hope is lost, Tramp swoops in to save the day. With his quick thinking and resourcefulness, Tramp orchestrates a daring escape through the busy streets, showcasing his street-smart survival skills. This scene not only highlights Tramp's bravery but also introduces the budding romance between him and Lady, setting the stage for their heartwarming love story.

Tramp's character is portrayed as a lovable rogue with a kind heart. While he may appear rough around the edges, Tramp possesses a deep sense of loyalty and compassion. He is a protector of the less fortunate and understands the struggles of life on the streets. Tramp's experiences have made him wise and perceptive, allowing him to navigate the world with a unique perspective. As the film unfolds, Tramp's endearing personality and devotion to Lady showcase his transformation from a street-smart wanderer to a loyal and devoted companion.

Trusty

Trusty, the wise and experienced Bloodhound from Disney's "Lady and the Tramp," is a beloved character who brings wisdom, guidance, and a touch of nostalgia to the story. As an old and respected member of the community, Trusty plays a significant role in supporting and mentoring Lady and Tramp throughout their adventures.

With his deep, rumbling voice and sagely demeanor, Trusty serves as a voice of reason and a source of knowledge. He often imparts valuable life lessons and shares stories from his own past, offering guidance and reassurance to the younger dogs. Trusty's role as an elder figure adds depth and emotional resonance to the narrative, showcasing the importance of wisdom gained through experience.

Despite his age, Trusty retains a strong sense of determination and loyalty. He demonstrates unwavering dedication to his friends and is always ready to lend a helping paw when needed. Trusty's steadfastness and dependability make him a pillar of support and a reliable companion for Lady and Tramp.

Trusty's character represents the significance of tradition, wisdom, and the passing down of knowledge from one generation to the next. His role in "Lady and the Tramp" reminds viewers of the importance of learning from those who came before us, cherishing their wisdom, and honoring the lessons they impart.

Beyond his role as a mentor, Trusty's presence adds a touch of charm and nostalgia to the story. His distinctive appearance and endearing mannerisms capture the essence of the wise, old Bloodhound archetype, creating a character that is both lovable and memorable.

Underdog

Underdog, the beloved superhero canine in the TV cartoon "Underdog," is a charismatic and courageous character with a secret identity. By day, he is a humble and mild-mannered shoeshine boy named Shoeshine, but when trouble strikes, he transforms into the crime-fighting Underdog. Clad in his iconic blue and red costume, Underdog possesses superpowers that he uses to protect the city from evildoers and save the day. His charming and endearing personality, coupled with his unwavering determination, make him a beloved hero to both children and adults alike.

One of the most memorable aspects of Underdog's character is his humorous and often self-deprecating nature. Despite his incredible superpowers, Underdog's humble personality shines through as he often finds himself in comical and clumsy situations. Whether it's his tendency to accidentally cause chaos or his amusingly dramatic declarations of his secret identity, Underdog's lighthearted and humorous demeanor adds a delightful touch to the show. However, when it's time to fight crime, Underdog's bravery and unwavering sense of justice take center stage, proving that even the most unlikely heroes can make a difference.

Underdog's character embodies the classic trope of an underdog rising to the occasion. Despite his unassuming alter ego, Shoeshine, Underdog's true strength lies in his indomitable spirit and the belief that anyone can become a hero. Through his adventures and escapades, Underdog teaches valuable lessons about courage, perseverance, and the power of doing what's right. His iconic catchphrase, "There's no need to fear, Underdog is here!" resonates with audiences, inspiring them to face their own challenges with determination and a sense of humor.

Verdell

Verdell, the adorable Brussels Griffon in the movie "As Good as It Gets," stole the hearts of audiences with his scene-stealing performance. As the constant companion of the grumpy and obsessive-compulsive writer Melvin Udall, played by Jack Nicholson, Verdell serves as a source of comfort and unexpected connection. With his expressive eyes and lovable personality, Verdell adds a touch of warmth and levity to the film, becoming a symbol of unconditional love and friendship.

One memorable scene featuring Verdell occurs when Melvin reluctantly agrees to care for the dog in his neighbor's absence. Despite his initial reluctance and disdain for the small canine, Melvin gradually forms a bond with Verdell. This bond is beautifully portrayed through moments of tenderness and vulnerability, where Verdell's presence brings out a softer side of Melvin. The interactions between Melvin and Verdell showcase the transformative power of companionship and the profound impact that a loyal and loving pet can have on even the most guarded hearts.

White Fang

White Fang, the eponymous character of Jack London's novel, is a captivating and resilient wolfdog who embarks on a remarkable journey through the unforgiving wilderness. As the story unfolds, White Fang's experiences serve as a lens through which readers explore themes of survival, instinct, and the complex relationship between humans and animals.

White Fang's character is shaped by his dual nature, blending the instincts and resilience of a wild wolf with the influence and interaction with humans. His early life in the harsh and brutal wilderness instills in him a fierce independence and an innate understanding of the natural world. As the story progresses, White Fang encounters human civilization, leading to an exploration of his adaptability and the intricate dynamics between human society and the untamed wild.

Through White Fang's experiences, readers are invited to reflect on the primal instincts that drive us, as well as the profound impact of nurture versus nature. The novel explores the transformative power of love, trust, and companionship as White Fang navigates both the cruelty and compassion that he encounters in the human world.

White Fang's character embodies the strength and resilience of animals, captivating readers with his journey of survival and growth. His complex and evolving relationship with humans offers a window into the human capacity for both cruelty and kindness, prompting us to question our own treatment of the natural world and our responsibility towards other species.

Wishbone

Wishbone, the titular character of the show, is an imaginative Jack Russell Terrier who resides in the fictional town of Oakdale, Texas, alongside his owner Joe Talbot. With a boundless imagination, Wishbone embarks on daydreams where he assumes the roles of lead characters from beloved works of classic literature. Known as "the little dog with a big imagination," Wishbone's unique ability to bring stories to life sets him apart. While only the viewers and the characters within his daydreams can hear Wishbone speak, those characters perceive him as the famous character he is currently portraying, rather than as a dog.

One of the most remarkable aspects of Wishbone's character was his uncanny ability to seamlessly weave himself into the plots of classic novels. From adventures with Sherlock Holmes to embodying the daring spirit of Robin Hood, Wishbone's escapades offered a creative and entertaining way to introduce young audiences to the timeless works of literature. Wishbone's vibrant personality and his ability to capture the essence of beloved characters brought an extra layer of magic to each episode, fostering a love of reading and a sense of adventure.

Winn-Dixie

Winn-Dixie, the endearing canine protagonist in the novel "Because of Winn-Dixie" by Kate DiCamillo, is a lovable stray dog who brings about profound changes in the life of a young girl named Opal. Winn-Dixie's appearance may be scruffy and unkempt, but his kind eyes and wagging tail instantly capture the hearts of those he encounters. It is through his companionship and unwavering loyalty that Winn-Dixie helps heal the emotional wounds of those around him, creating lasting connections and fostering a sense of belonging in a small Southern town.

Winn-Dixie's character is portrayed as gentle, intuitive, and full of curiosity. From the moment Opal first meets him in a supermarket, the bond between the two is instant. Winn-Dixie becomes Opal's confidant and steadfast companion, providing her with a sense of comfort and understanding. As the story unfolds, it becomes evident that Winn-Dixie possesses a unique ability to bring people together. Through his interactions with the various eccentric characters in the town, Winn-Dixie acts as a catalyst for forgiveness, acceptance, and friendship. His playful antics and contagious enthusiasm create moments of joy and laughter, and his presence serves as a reminder of the transformative power of love and compassion in our lives.

Zero

Zero, the ethereal ghost dog in the film "The Nightmare Before Christmas," is a spectral and endearing character that adds a touch of otherworldly charm to the story. With his glowing pumpkin nose and floating form, Zero serves as the loyal and devoted companion to Jack Skellington, the Pumpkin King. Despite his ephemeral nature, Zero's unwavering loyalty and gentle spirit make him a beloved presence in the dark and whimsical world of Halloween Town.

Zero's character is portrayed as both mischievous and caring. While he may not possess the traditional qualities of a typical dog, his presence brings comfort and joy to those around him. Zero's glowing nose acts as a guiding light, leading Jack through the eerie landscapes and dark passages of the film. His spectral form allows him to navigate the ethereal realm effortlessly, providing a sense of wonder and enchantment. Zero's playful interactions with Jack and his dedication to helping his friend uncover the true meaning of Christmas demonstrate his unwavering loyalty and his belief in the power of love and friendship.

Despite Zero's lack of words, his expressive eyes and gentle movements convey a range of emotions, evoking both sympathy and adoration from viewers. Zero's character serves as a reminder that true companionship extends beyond physical boundaries and appearances. He embodies the essence of loyalty, friendship, and the unbreakable bond between a devoted pet and their owner. Through his presence in "The Nightmare Before Christmas," Zero captivates audiences with his spectral charm and leaves a lasting impression of the importance of love, loyalty, and the magic of the holiday season.